THE FUSION

The Fusion

Israel in a Biblical End-Time Scenario

IAN HEARD

WIPF & STOCK · Eugene, Oregon

THE FUSION
Israel in a Biblical End-Time Scenario

Wipf & Stock
An Imprint of Wipf and Stock Publishers
199 W. 8th Ave., Suite 3
Eugene, OR 97401

www.wipfandstock.com

PAPERBACK ISBN: 979-8-3852-1312-2
HARDCOVER ISBN: 979-8-3852-1313-9
EBOOK ISBN: 979-8-3852-1314-6

04/18/24

Contents

Prologue

And there will be one flock and one shepherd.

JESUS, IN JOHN 10:16

IN OUR TIMES IT is probably not an exaggeration to say that Bible teaching and speculation among Christians about Israel, "end-times," and the return of Jesus Christ has become in some quarters akin to an industry.

Some have been "left behind" by some popular and imaginative teachings, while others spend probably more time than they ought on hearing what this teacher or that "prophetic" voice is saying.

It is not my desire to add to the confusing cacophony of sounds.

In contemplating passages like Zech 12–14 and others, we are confronted with mysterious, prophesied events, some of which seem impractical, if not impossible.

However, when we examine the already fulfilled foretellings of biblical prophets, we see that in the chaos, twists, and turns of history, God has ways of bringing about things that have always appeared impractical or impossible.

We see those fulfillments in that clearest kind of sight—hindsight; but to God, foresight and hindsight or after-sight are one and the same!

How could anyone have known that a decree was to go out from Caesar Augustus for a census, under which citizens had to travel to their home towns and register? What Caesar didn't know was that he was being instrumental in the fulfillment of the prophetic word of God through Micah:

> But you, Bethlehem Ephrathah,
> Though you are little among the thousands of Judah,
> Yet out of you shall come forth to Me
> The One to be Ruler in Israel,
> Whose goings forth are from of old,
> From everlasting. (Mic 5:2)

Consider, for example, the number of times the Gospel writers and Matthew particularly say, "That it might be fulfilled which was spoken by the prophet." Or—consider Peter at Pentecost in that epiphanous moment of recognition, "*This is that* which was spoken by the prophet Joel" (Acts 2:16; cf. Joel 2:28–32).

During a visit to Israel in late 2019 I witnessed a Jewish re-enactment of the ancient tabernacle ritual on a site with a life-size replica of the Israelites' wilderness tabernacle.

As I read back into the realistic ritual the Christian revelation of the now-fulfilled-in-Christ meaning of it all, I began to visualize a situation where Jewish eyes and understanding might become opened and awakened to that fulfillment. And, not that only—but also a situation where the eyes of many Christians might be opened fully to the amazing visual earthly drama God provided for Israel (and all people) in both tabernacle and later temple, which illustrate truths and realities that exist in another realm: the heavenly realm. That holy of holies compartment represented within a tent on earth the otherwise inaccessible presence of the Holy God. Here, the high priest entered once a year—but not without blood—as an expiating yet temporary sacrifice and offering for sin.

Some of Israel's great prophets, such as Ezekiel or Daniel or Zechariah, caught glimpses of these heavenly realities, of which the earthly buildings and accoutrements were but types and shadows. Spiritually minded and awake Jews perceived their calling and responsibility—and also knew that the outward and physical things pointed to things both deeper and farther out. And also knew that the great, large heart of Yahweh extended to *all* nations.

On the matter of the seismic shifts in Jewish and Christian disposition I mentioned above, consider these words from the New Testament. The first is from the mouth of Caiaphas, the high priest at the time of Jesus's trial and crucifixion—and recorded and understood as prophetic by John:

> And one of them, Caiaphas, being high priest that year, said to them, "You know nothing at all, nor do you consider that it is expedient for us that one man should die for the people, and not that the whole nation should perish." This he did not say on his own authority; but being high priest that year he prophesied that Jesus would die for the nation, and not for that nation only, but also *that He would gather together in one the children of God* who were scattered abroad. (John 11:52)

Then, too, we have the words of Jesus recorded in John 10:14–16:

> I am the good shepherd; and I know My sheep, and am known by My own. As the Father knows Me, even so I know the Father; and I lay down My life for the sheep. And other sheep I have which are not of this fold; them also I must bring, and they will hear My voice; *and there will be one flock and one shepherd.*

One flock and one shepherd! What I propose in what you are about to read is that God has given us, in the Pharisee Saul of Tarsus who became Paul the Christian apostle, an image and "type" of post-Calvary Israel, turning eventually from Old to New. From Moses to Christ!

CHAPTER 1

Saul of Tarsus: The Archetype?

THERE IS A BIBLICAL PATTERN of foreshadowing, of "types" and "antitypes"—the shadow appears first, followed by a more total expression or fullness. Here is an illustration I have used elsewhere that may help:

When you are standing near the corner of a building and the sun is low, you may see on the ground the shadow of another person approaching the corner from another direction before they actually appear. At the moment, they are out of sight to you, but you may see their shadow, and you know that a person will soon appear. The shadow may provide more or less detail depending on the person and light conditions, but you will have certainty of both their direction and of their soon-to-be fully realized arrival. When the person represented by the shadow is known to us, we may well recognize some characteristics—say, an Afro hairstyle or a particular rolling gait—before we actually see them.

So it is with the types and shadows in the Old Testament, which signal an arriving reality.

They come to us with varying amounts of detail, sometimes more specific than others, but they do make certain the arrival of a reality ahead. Once we know the One whose shadow keeps appearing in the Old Testament we recognize and anticipate the arrival much more readily.

Here are some familiar examples: Melchizedek blessing Abraham foreshadows Jesus Christ, as do King David and his son, Solomon. Abraham, Moses, and the prophets, as well as many people and incidents, offer types and foreshadowings of Messiah and coming salvation and of the Christian life. The tabernacle and its furnishings and rituals foreshadow him; the feasts of Israel are types and shadows that have been, or are being, fulfilled; for example, Passover was fulfilled in the shedding of the blood of Jesus, the Passover Lamb of God who took away the sin of the world, and fifty days later, the Jewish Feast of Pentecost was consummated with the outpouring of Holy Spirit on the believers in Jerusalem. Paul informs us in 1 Cor 10 that both the sea and the cloud experienced by Israel foreshadowed two baptisms for believers. In short, the Old Testament is a mother lode, a gloriously rich vein of opal truth awaiting consummation in the New. In fact, it can be said that the New is an unfolding actualization of spiritual realities whose seeds were planted in the Old. Or, to return to the opal analogy, like those dull, buried stones awaiting the arrival of a light that reveals their priceless opalescence! The old saying is valid: "The New is in the Old, concealed; the Old is in the New, revealed."

Since such foreshadowings or "types" in what we call the old covenant were instituted and used by God to point ahead to future fulfillments and to engender expectation and hope—is it also possible that some significant new covenant events are also pointers and signs to enlarged and yet-to-be-realized events in his purposes?

The resurrection of Yeshua is the harbinger of a far larger eventuality—the great resurrection of all people to their eternal destiny. The Holy Spirit coming upon Yeshua visibly at his baptism is a type and foreshadowing of the descent of the Spirit on the church at Pentecost and on believers throughout time. And of course, what is called the communion, instituted by Jesus, is not only to be taken in remembrance but also to point us forward to the day of its consummation when, as Jesus said, "I drink it new with you in my Father's kingdom" (Matt 26:29).

While there is no further or additional covenant to come of which I am aware, there is another age to come of which Jesus and the apostles had plenty to say. For example, Jesus said that in the infinite resurrection reality to come we neither marry nor are given in marriage—there is only one marriage there—that of the Lamb with his bride. All believers will find extraordinary consummation in that! Indeed, since marriage here is intended to be the means for reproduction, it can easily be assumed that the new marriage there (of the Lamb to his bride) has the same intention—productivity!

There is much in the new covenant that points to the infinite and timeless life to come—but why should there not also be types and shadows in this age in which we exist, of things to come to fulfillment either before or after its end?

Further examples could perhaps be found in the stoning of that first martyr, Stephen, and certainly in Peter's vision on the rooftop of the house of Simon the tanner in Joppa. These serve as kinds of prototypes. Martyrdom can be expected, and there have been many martyrs since Stephen. Certainly, God uses singular dramatic events to point to principles that apply more widely than to one occurrence.

Here then is the question: Are some significant New Testament events intended to point to and to raise expectation of larger fulfillments? Are they embryonic—and in fact, prophetic?

Saul of Tarsus?

I am now particularly thinking of the dramatic conversion of Saul of Tarsus, that fervent Pharisee, offended and inflamed with wrath over what the followers of Yeshua were claiming: the preposterous belief that Yeshua of Nazareth was Mashiach (Messiah) and had risen from the dead! But God had a mighty plan for this man, Saul, who railed against these Christians, had them killed, and had aided and abetted Stephen's death.

Sovereignly, the God Saul was persecuting interrupted his murderous trajectory on his way to Damascus "breathing out threatenings and slaughter" (Acts 9:1) against Christians! Saul, after a great repentance and conversion, became Paul, the magnificent apostle to the gentiles. It was a seismic event, the effects of which reverberate today. It was a turning in an instant under the sovereign hand of the Almighty. With that Light that shone about him, brighter than the sun—that penetrating, inescapable Light with its accompanying voice—came instant revelation and dawning of truth! And of his enormous error!

"Saul, why do you persecute *me?*" was the question brought by the voice into the heart of Saul!

The very last thing this zealot would ever think of doing was blaspheming or speaking against the God he believed he was serving—and now this very One speaks to cause Saul to realize that was indeed his sin! To persecute the church was to persecute God!

The turning was as opposite and polar as East is to West, as negative current to positive, as night to day! And it occurred almost in the blink of an eye.

My following question then is: Was the dramatic conversion of Saul a prophetic portent—an embryonic and prophetic sign of, and for, the future of his nation?

Is it possible that in embryo, Saul represents a swathe of national Israel who likewise will undergo a climactic and profound turning to Mashiach Yeshua just as that of Saul, the archetype?

A Larger Meaning?

Was Saul becoming Paul a hint, a shadow, and "type" of things to come for Israel under the sovereign hand of God? Are there any clues or hints in Scripture that might help us? My conviction is yes, so we'll begin by considering the following from the great apostle himself:

> Brethren, my heart's desire and prayer to God for Israel is that they may be saved. For I bear them witness that *they have a zeal for God, but not according to knowledge. For they, being ignorant of God's righteousness, and seeking to establish their own righteousness,* have not submitted to the righteousness of God. For Christ is the end

of-the-law-for-righteousness to everyone who believes. (Rom 10:1–4 [hyphenation added])

You can see clearly how this description of Saul's kinfolk springs so naturally from Saul's own savage zealotry and self-righteousness, followed by his out-of-the-ordinary experience. He was, effectively, describing himself and was looking at his people through the lens of his own experience; as he had been, so are they. He had been the epitome of a "righteousness-by-law" bigot and zealot, striving to establish (and prove) his own righteousness. The idea that the righteousness he sought was something that had now been won for him by this Yeshua—that it was something to be received, not achieved—had been utter anathema to his mind. In view of this, his deepest yearning and prayer are that those who had a similar zeal to that which had possessed him might be saved—even as he had been. That was Rom 10:1–4. Now let's consider Rom 11:1–3:

> I say then, has God cast away His people? Certainly not! *For I also am an Israelite, of the seed of Abraham, of the tribe of Benjamin. God has not cast away His people whom He foreknew.* Or do you not know what the Scripture says of Elijah, how he pleads with God against Israel, saying, *"Lord, they have killed Your prophets and torn down Your altars,* and I alone am left, and they seek my life." But what does the divine response say to him? *"I have reserved for Myself seven thousand* men who have not bowed the knee to Baal." Even so then, *at this present time there is a remnant* according to the election of grace. And if by grace, then it is no longer of works; otherwise, grace is no longer grace. But if it is of works, it is no longer grace; otherwise, work is no longer work.
>
> What then? Israel has not obtained what it seeks; *but the elect have obtained it*, and the rest were blinded. Just as it is written:
>
> God has given them a spirit of stupor,
> Eyes that they should not see.
> And ears that they should not hear,
> To this very day.

5

Reserved—Not Rejected!

Again, Paul is using himself as the archetype—casting himself as the very example of *non-rejection* and of the Jew *not* cast away! If God rejected all Israel, then he surely had to reject me, the quintessential Hebrew—of the seed of Abraham and of the tribe of Benjamin (Binyamin—"son of the right hand"—of Jacob)! Instead, he *chose* me, even when I was opposed to him! I am elect!

Later in the chapter (v. 16) he says, "For if the *firstfruit* is holy, the lump is also holy; and if the root is holy, so are the branches."

We must, I believe, keep in mind that Paul has based these paragraphs found in Rom 11 on the foundational argument (of v. 1) that it is quite clear that Israel has not been rejected because he—as an Israelite and as a "type" of the whole—has so manifestly not been rejected. As it is for him, as prototype (or firstfruit), so will it be for the whole! Everything that follows v. 1 has this statement as its premise.

Paul then uses the illustration of Elijah and those "seven thousand" whom God had *reserved* for himself. As we understand, the numeral seven usually typifies completion or fullness in the Scriptures, and those seven thousand are, in my view, a foreshadowing of what Paul calls in Rom 11 "all Israel," having already qualified that cohort as those who do not persist in an attitude of unbelief.[1] More on this in chapter 10.

Returning to Paul's use of the word *firstfruit* in v. 16, consider this: in v. 13 he says that as the apostle to the gentiles, he is magnifying his *ministry of provocation* to his own people. That is, his ministry of the gospel to the gentiles, as he has said in v. 11, "provokes" the Jews to jealousy! It is in this context—speaking of himself in the role of provocateur, that he then describes himself as *firstfruit* of his peoples' "acceptance." Remember, he has been comparing his own situation and experience with that of his people, Israel. And so, he says (paraphrased), "If I, as the example and

---

1. See Rom 11:23: "And they also, *if they do not continue in unbelief,* will be grafted in, for God is able to graft them in again."

firstfruit, am holy, then the whole lump can be seen in the same way—holy!"

Paul then speaks of root, branches, and fruit, which are, of course, entirely different parts: the root being the foundation and source, and the others the outgrowth and product. In my view, Paul is here referring to Abraham and the patriarchs as the root; then those of Israel who were obedient prior to Calvary and the resurrection, as the branches arising from that root—and then his Jewish self, as a prototype of a coming bounty of fruit among his people. His argument appears to be that what has appeared in the prototype or firstfruit will be manifested in the whole lump.

Interestingly, in another place Paul also describes himself as "one born out of due time" (1 Cor 15:8) when he speaks of himself among those who were eyewitnesses of the risen Christ. On that Damascus road, Saul had become a belated eyewitness.

Will many of the Jewish people, like Paul the firstfruits, also become late "beholders" of the risen Christ—they too as post-term children? I am more and more persuaded so.

There's More . . .

Yes, there is more, so we should consider too what Paul gives us in 1 Tim 1:15–16:

> This is a faithful saying and worthy of all acceptance, that Christ Jesus came into the world to save sinners, of whom I am chief. However, for this reason I obtained mercy, that *in me first* Jesus Christ might show all long-suffering, *as a pattern* to those who are going to believe on Him for everlasting life.

Yes, he was primarily to be the great apostle to the gentiles,[2] but consider this: Was not this also the primary call of Israel—to be a light to the "goyim"—the nations? That they might see, and seeing—come? Yes, come to the Light! In the old covenant God's method was essentially "come and see"; *see* the model he had set

2. See Rom 1:5 and Gal 1:16, for example.

in the world. In the new, our commission is primarily "go and tell," but there must also be a winsomeness and an attractiveness in the church for the world to desire to come and see.

In Saul of Tarsus then, we have the quintessential Israelite, seeking, like many of his people, righteousness by the law, rejecting the idea of righteousness being possible by any other means—and especially that of faith in an already killed and risen again Mashiach. In Saul we have fleshly zeal that sees as virtuous the repudiation and stamping out of this "new way." In Saul we see, too, the near impossibility of conversion from entrenched cultural and religious zeal by intellectual argument alone. His religious and cultural heritage along with his prodigious intellect and Pharisaic doctrinal knowledge of Mosaic law and the Scriptures made that so. Here is a Jew with a huge investment in his learning and in ensuring that heresies were eliminated. Too big an investment of life and time to discuss with, let alone be persuaded by, these Christians. And yet, certainly something affected him deeply in the way he saw Stephen die and heard his dying words. And then? And then, the encounter! What human argument and intellectual reasoning could never do with a Saul of Tarsus, a meeting with the Risen One mid-trajectory certainly did!

It is my hope and certainly my prayer that, just as it occurred in the life of Saul of Tarsus as the prototype and indeed archetype, so it will occur in the life of "all" Israel—a dramatic and even sudden epiphany in which the Light shines "round about them" and their trajectory is changed as they collectively cry with Saul of Tarsus, "Who are you, Lord?"

CHAPTER 2

The Abraham/Melchizedek Ideal

ABRAHAM, THE FATHER and progenitor of our faith, in his encounter with the prototype priest/king Melchizedek was an early clue to the plan. That ordained meeting provides an inkling, not unlike the preliminary sketch for a painting, the detail of which would be filled in as history unfolded.

In that meeting, recorded in Gen 14, Abraham the obedient seeker is representative of those willing to leave behind inferior attachments to set out in obedience to the call of Elohim to seek the deepest attachment a heart can find. In it, he is brought into dynamic encounter with the man who stood as Elohim's representative. We know little of Melchizedek, yet Moses and later David and then the author of Hebrews understood him to be acting as an earthly intermediary, as "priest of the Most High God."[1]

It provides an idea in embryo. It is the genesis, the prototype, of a principle by which God will work to call and separate a people to himself—and indeed, how he works in the lives of seekers. Those who heed the quiet, inner voice that calls to better things (and who are willing to recognize it as the answer to deepest need) will indeed . . . find!

---

1. See Gen 14:18; Ps 110; Heb 7:1.

Called from—and to . . .

We are not just called *to* something: the call *to* something is, by necessity, a call *from* another thing. Abraham would not be shown what he was called to until he dealt with the "from" matter; God said, "*Leave . . .* and I will show you" (Gen 12:1). He was not at ease in Mesopotamia for God had begun to tug at his heart. There came the sense that he was here for a purpose different and greater than raising sheep and cattle only, as necessary as that was. It was the unease, disquiet, and uncertainty about identity and purpose that in moments of night thought may come to every human heart—calling it to reach out to touch concreteness and certainty. The sense that I have yet something to come into—a place of "arrival." Of course, there comes a lying voice too; that of the enemy of all good, who can shout quite loudly. That voice says that certainty will be found over here . . . or over there. It is hoped that by shouting, the quieter, insistent, true heart call may be overwhelmed. It is hoped that it will be far easier to capitulate and respond to the strident voice. Yet in the silence of the night or the aloneness of certain times, it can also be known that what is loudest is only so because it is also false!

There, within and deep down is the desire for our true and ultimate sense of "who-ness" and "why-ness." And so, the loud voice insists that of course these will be discovered in all kinds of material, visible places and things, or with all kinds of people, amusements, and activities—yet they turn out to be vanities. No question, some could be good and legitimate pursuits that provide a measure of pleasure and joy. But they are temporary and yield nothing like the satisfied totality intended for us—yes, each of us—by the One who made us for himself and for a specific reality.

Truth is, we are made for eternity, and what we produce here in this time-and-space realm can indeed be of eternal value and quality! Or—it can contribute merely to the rubbish pile of temporal and temporary things bound for destruction. God has in mind for each one works and contributions that build something for eternity. Those are the works Jesus told us about and of which

Paul wrote when he said, "For we are *God's* handiwork, created in Christ Jesus to do good works, which God *prepared in advance* for us to do" (Eph 2:10 NIV). That is where our "who-ness" resides. It is hidden there awaiting discovery as we incline hearts toward *him* and away from self-voice and the other loud voices.

Our selfhood is not found—cannot be found—in our own kingdom or just in our own "idea," because we are in fact, *his* idea, created *for* something. That "something" becomes found, ironically and counterintuitively, in becoming lost; lost to our idea and lost to our plan to discover ourselves, to be found in the distinctly intended place within his plan, fulfilling a specific and self-actualizing allotment! There, a sweet, comfortable, and peaceful sense of identity clothes us like a tailored garment. We become clothed and at home—not unlike the once-demonized Gadarene of Luke 8:35![2]

Of course, as life stretches out, many people tend to become inured to the call. The practiced denial of that "voice" and deliberate silencing of it are an open invitation to other voices and persuasions to appear more attractive and more likely to reward. There is a shell and then a concretion formed by practiced denial that prevents penetration of spiritual truth and light but lets in the sounds and appeal of the world and the flesh. For some, especially those who have achieved a measure of success and for whom the "lines have fallen in pleasant places" (Ps 16:6), to use the psalmist's phrase, complacency often rules. "Just give me my . . . (insert here favorite occupations or preoccupations: career, business, travel, sport, hobbies, family, relationships, influence, movies, music, plays, etc.), and I'm perfectly happy."

What is not recognized is that any or all of these—not intrinsically wrong in themselves—fall immeasurably short of the best that is available, because it is not possible for anything in the material world to provide what is needed for our completion. If I am trusting "things" to produce the completed "me"—I am selling myself short. It is often those very "things" that too easily blind

2. "Then they went out to see what had happened, and came to Jesus, and found the man from whom the demons had departed, sitting at the feet of Jesus, clothed and in his right mind. And they were afraid."

me to the real Source; to the only One whence that for which I most yearn can come. There is an irony here, because it is from that Source that all legitimate "things" not only become ordered into their proper place but also acquire a tangible "redemptive lift." As an old hymn writer expressed it:

> Heav'n above is deeper blue,
> Earth around is sweeter green,
> Something lives in ev'ry hue
> Christless eyes have never seen:
> Birds in song his glories show,
> Flow'rs with richer beauties shine
> Since I know, as now I know,
> I am His and He is mine.[3]

Yes, there exists a kind of second-level satisfaction, but its lack of validity is revealed as its "shine" fades and a new or next "thing" is desired to provide what has now evaporated. As these temporary "shine producers" march in succession through a life, they produce, increment by increment, a tough enamel over any soft spots whereby it may have been "vulnerable" to the true voice and the true call! Through practice, people arrive by capitulation at a philosophy that is agnostic to truth. They come to believe it cannot really be known; or that "this" (meaning a kind of somewhat enjoyable or making-the-best-of-it existence) is all that can be expected. Alternatively, they may embrace the idea that there may be an afterlife, but if so, being as good as the next person or perhaps a little better is qualification enough to make it into the "good" part of that life! (Which is a bit like answering the question "How fast must you run if a bear is chasing you?" with the answer "Just a little bit faster than your colleague!")

What "Everyman" is called *from* is all those attempts to find their consummation and "homeness" in places other than in God! The call is to discover it in the only One from whom it can come. Abraham was used as an exemplar: a prototype to emulate. There were others before him, too, like Enoch, but God chose Abraham

---

3. Wade Robinson, "Loved with Everlasting Love" (https://hymnary.org/text/loved_with_everlasting_love), st. 2.

to demonstrate the principles and the way—and through him to raise up a people who would model that way.

That portentous meeting with Melchizedek was extraordinary—and prescient. It showed what Elohim intended: man on a journey away from what cannot ever answer, into a growing encounter with the God who does answer; man in relationship with him. Man in a giving/receiving relationship wherein the lesser serves and worships the greater and, in so doing, finds provision and purpose and expansion released to him.

Having been called *from* something, Abraham was now beginning to see the *to* into which he was being called and led. A new way of living in dependence, not on things tangible that the many looked to, but on the Living One, the Yahweh Yireh[4] of Mount Moriah!

That is what the encounter does. When anyone seeks and therefore finds the One represented on that far back day by Melchizedek, they are transformed forever into people who depend on a new and living way. The way of dependence on the Lord of Abraham!

It was but the foreshadowing of what could be: a new and better way arriving among us on an incomparable rescue mission.

Meantime . . .

---

4. Gen 22:14: "And Abraham called the name of the place Yahweh Yireh (the LORD will provide)"

CHAPTER 3

Earth's Special Place

THE TITLE OF THIS CHAPTER is intended to invoke two meanings: the first being that Earth occupies a special place within creation and within the heart of the Creator, and second, that within the Earth there is a special place standing as the epicenter of God's plan!

The Earth was designed and created for a special creation—mankind. That this is so is self-evident but nonetheless is not believed by those whose disposition is to, well . . . not believe. Unbelief has become the default position of so many, because it suits them to (temporarily) avoid the ramifications of belief—and of dependence. For belief immediately implies (and imposes) an accountability they are not yet willing to embrace, although—fact is—whether they choose to believe or not they remain account-able, as that "day" of which the Bible speaks so often will reveal.

There is little need to spend time here on the overwhelming witness that this is true of this tiny speck, floating as it does in the unimaginable numbers of other bodies, none of which come close to emulating Earth. To the heart that is deliberate in unbelief this must be dismissed as tosh. To the heart disposed to truth it is but one of the things in which the voice and the call of the one known as the Almighty are heard.

The Place

But, upon this special planet there is also a special place. In fact, since the patriarchs and throughout the Bible it became known as HaMakom, the Place, or the Site.[1] That God's plan for the special creation made for his special people should have a special place should not come as a surprise. It is where the story of mankind began, where it culminated in the one called Yeshua, and where it will be finalized.

Of course, I'm speaking of Jerusalem, but more particularly of the southward ridge of Mount Moriah on which stood the ancient Salem, later Jebus and then the city of David and Zion. In this author's view this was also the location of Eden, the place where God first walked with and communed with his most glorious created-in-his-image being, near the spring known as Gihon. Gihon: the fabled siphon or karst-type spring whose name means "gushing up," once capable of thrusting up large quantities of water under pressure—and the reason the early settlements were there. That spring was to become the biblical "type" for the water of life—living water, flowing from the presence of God. It is the designated site known as Zion, around which God's plan and redemptive activity centered—from Abraham and Isaac to Melchizedek to Jacob and onward through Moses and the prophets and David and Solomon, even to the Jerusalem of our Mashiach Yeshua's day![2]

I am making a point of the significance of the Place (HaMakom) because some today are inclined to diminish its importance in God's plan. This is particularly true of those Christians who characterize themselves by belief in replacement theology—that is, that the Jewish nation has today been replaced by the church. In this theology the Jews as a people have "done their dash," and while individuals may come to the Savior, God has no further plans for them as a people. This is not a view I can endorse as I do believe

---

1. See Ian Heard, *The Temple Quest: Biblical Evidence for the True Location* (N.p.: Smashwords, 2022; eBook); and Ian Heard, *The Place: HaMakom; Where Jerusalem's Temples Stood* (Eugene, OR: Wipf and Stock, 2015).

2. See Heard, *Temple Quest*; and Heard, *Place*.

that there is yet to be a great turning among them—and even as a people. One cannot witness their miraculous resurrection as a nation in May 1948, followed by their extraordinary victory in the Six-Day War of 1967, followed by their flowering since, and deny a sovereign hand on their destiny.

So—we have a special planet on which there is a special place, and there is, related to that place, a special people. Let me underline for you the importance of the place known as HaMakom.

It had been chosen by God to be the place:

- Where Abraham encountered Melchizedek
- Where Abraham was directed to relinquish Isaac
- Where Jacob had his dream and called it Beit-El (Bethel), or House of God
- Where God told Moses they would worship when they entered the land
- Where David placed his tent and the ark at Gihon in the city of David
- Of which Jeremiah spoke many times
- Of the locus of his great plan—where he would reside among his people, around which he would reveal the plan, where Mashiach Yeshua would be crucified and rise from death, from which the gospel would sound out, and to which Mashiach will return. Its nickname was HaMakom.

Still Special?

You can see then the importance of the Place in the grand scheme.

Here then is a question. If the city of David, Zion—the city wrested millennia ago from the hands of the Jebusites—whose name meant "downtreaders"—was transformed into the city of God over which Yeshua wept; if it has been forever rejected by God, why is it the site to which Yeshua promised to return?

You see, it remains in his heart. It remains the locus, whether we like the idea or not; until the consummation of all things, that place and its people have a role.

What Jesus had to say of Jerusalem towards the end, as recorded by Matthew, is of utmost importance. Here it is:

> O Jerusalem, Jerusalem, the one who kills the prophets and stones those who are sent to her! How often I wanted to gather your children together, as a hen gathers her chicks under her wings, but you were not willing! See! *Your house is left to you desolate;* for I say to you, you shall see Me no more *till* you say, "Blessed is He who comes in the name of the LORD!" (Matt 23:37–39)

Now, the word translated "desolate" here is the Greek word ἔρημος (*eremos*). It comes into English in our word *eremite*, meaning a hermit or one living alone, isolated and solitary. This describes perfectly what I believe Yeshua meant. He had again and again wanted to gather her, that is, Jerusalem's children, protectively, as a hen her chicks, *"but you were not willing,"* he said (v. 37). The time for those overtures was now over *until* the day when they eventually (and willingly) say, "Blessed is He who comes in the name of the LORD." (We will return to this important statement from Yeshua later. Let it suffice for the moment to recognize both the significance and the strategic importance of the location known as HaMakom, the Place, in earth's history.)

So, we see the word *desolate* used in a way that is intended to convey the opposite of chicks being gathered and protected beneath the safety and intimacy of the wings of the hen. They are, for the moment, somewhat at the mercy of predators and other dangers.

As we know, ancient Israel after deliverance from Egypt, and due to their unbelief and disobedience, failed to enter what God was bringing them to. They brought upon themselves forty years of wilderness futility until the unbelieving generation had passed away. Today, they are in a similar "wilderness" due to unbelief and rejection of their Mashiach. However, just as in that forty-year wilderness chastening, God still cared for them, provided for them, and led them, so today his hand abides upon them during their blindness (Rom 11:25) until two things occur. The first is the completion of the gentile portion of the whole flock that Shepherd Yeshua is making up—and the second, until that which we read of in Zech 12:10 comes:

> And I will pour on the house of David and on the inhabitants of Jerusalem the Spirit of grace and supplication; then they will look on Me whom they pierced. Yes, they will mourn for Him as one mourns for his only son, and grieve for Him as one grieves for a firstborn.

CHAPTER 4

The Law: Interim yet Eternal!

So . . . while Father Ivrahim, or Abraham, exemplified God's required way of living, the way of faith—nevertheless the law became a necessity. Why? Because, as Paul told us, we needed a consciousness of sin, of its seriousness—and of the ramifications of lawless behavior. We needed a guardian or tutor to carry us through to the "arrival" of Mashiach.[1]

All our highways have signs. A proliferation of them, in fact, all intended to remind us how to behave. When we are either neglectfully or willfully speeding down the freeway at eighty miles per hour and a sign appears reminding us that the speed limit is sixty-five, what is its effect? It does not just inform; it also condemns! And at that point we must make a decision. Will I continue to take the risks of endangering lives and of receiving a penalty, or will I quickly be chastened and drop my speed to sixty-five or less? It would do me no good at all to introduce my own idea and standard by saying, "Well, today I'm doing eighty because it suits me, but tomorrow on the way home I'll do fifty-five all the way to compensate." Of course, we know that would not stand up before the magistrate, no matter how reasonable *we* considered it.

---

1. Gal 3:24, where the Greek word παιδαγωγός (*paidagogos*) literally means one who leads youths, or one charged with tutelage and discipline.

What is the problem here? The problem is that the law exists, external to me, to announce a requirement and to attempt to enforce my compliance. It is not an attitude of gracious and willing compliance written within and coming from me; it is something from outside me that cannot change what is in my heart. My heart may bitterly resent the sixty-five limit and rail against its stupidity. No amount of signs has any wherewithal to change that. It can't make my attitude good or different (or even reasonable and sensible). Its role is to inform; and when I am not compliant, it judges, revealing to me how wrong I am—and reveals that the "wrongness" is mine. I'd rather believe I can do as I please and make my own rules and offer all kinds of justification for doing so. Another and very different response the speed signs may elicit within is to become self-righteous about my diligent sixty-five miles per hour law keeping and carp about all the other terrible people who disregard it! This was what the Pharisees of Jesus's day did. It is the attitude in much of the righteousness-of-man virtue signaling and self-congratulation seen among politicians, in the arts, academia, and "woke" warriors of our day.

Issues of the Heart

In each scenario my attitude (my heart) is where the problem lies—and no matter how many sixty-five mph signs there may be, in each case I am preferring my own judgment and my own way. Further, I'll probably be angry if I'm caught and penalized! If only all those signs were able to change my attitude to one of desire for compliance—and even to delight *in* compliance! But they are powerless to do so. Imagine if all those signs and reminders were never required, because everyone's heart was right and desired only to do right? The only change the signs can effect is that brought about by coercion and threat of punishment. We all comply and become amenable once we see the flashing blue light!

This is what the law of Moses did and did well; it made sin evident—as Paul wrote, "It brought sin alive"[2]—and it also exposed my heart attitude.

A better and higher idea of a better and higher way was in train—and already being exemplified, but because we live in the realm of time and on its linearity, it had to await its spot on the line. But this higher and better way *was* always foreshadowed. In fact, its principle was, at all moments and all the way along (and above) the time line, both operable and accessible. It was there although hidden, so that those who believed could access it prospectively (as it were) through the One who was always "arriving" on his mission to instigate and make accessible to all the new way!

Hence David could take the bread of the presence in time of need because grace always stood behind and above the law, as will be discussed shortly in chapter 7. Thus, Samuel could say to Saul, "Has the LORD as great delight in burnt offerings and sacrifices, as in obeying the voice of the LORD? *Behold, to obey is better than sacrifice*, and to heed than the fat of rams" (1 Sam 15:23).

Or, what about the word of God through Hosea? "For I desire mercy and not sacrifice, And the knowledge of God more than burnt offerings" (Hos 6:6). And, of course, Ps 40:6, "Sacrifice and offering You did not desire; My ears You have opened. Burnt offering and sin offering You did not require." The opened ears of the psalmist recognized that it was a heart functioning in the obedience of faith that was the real necessity. Here it is again in Prov 21:3, "To do righteousness and justice is more acceptable to the LORD than sacrifice."

Indeed, once we begin to look, there are many references in the Old Testament, and we could cite Ps 50:7–23, where vv. 14 and 15 explain what the relationship is to be like—"Offer to God thanksgiving, and *pay your vows* to the Most High, call upon Me in the day of trouble; I will deliver you, and you shall glorify Me." And v. 23: "Whoever *offers praise* glorifies Me; And to him who orders his conduct aright I will show the salvation of God." Or

2. Rom 7:9: "When the commandment came, sin became alive, and I died." (NASB).

Ps 69:30–31, "I will praise the name of God with a song and will magnify Him with thanksgiving. This also shall please the LORD *better than an ox or bull.*"

These are but a few instances that show that for Lord Yahweh, what resided in and issued from a person's heart was as important, or more so, than outward formality and ritual. The form and ritual were there as the speed signs on the highway—to remind and pattern and train the heart in righteousness as well as to ensure that mankind was without excuse. They could not legitimately say, "Why didn't you tell me?" Both the commandment and the sacrifice were there as continual reminders of the offence and the seriousness of sin . . . a life had to be taken, a substitute die.

But . . . neither any one of those sacrifices nor the entire sum of them could ever "take away" sin and guilt. There was coming a once-for-all offering—one that would swallow them all; one that would indeed deal finally and efficaciously with all sin. The temporary ones all pointed forward to it, but "it" would fulfill, consummate, and therefore make obsolete all those that went before.

That is what John the Baptist saw when he pointed to Mashiach Yeshua, declaring, "Behold! The Lamb of God who *bears away* the sin of the whole world!" (John 1:29).

Until Yeshua dealt summarily with all of mankind's sin it had not been carried away. The scapegoat bearing sin into the wilderness in the old covenant was but an image pointing to the One who would summarily fulfill the "carrying away" of our trespasses. There are three quite different words used in the old covenant describing sin, and they are all used together in Ps 51 (as well as other places), where they are usually translated "iniquity," "transgression," and "sin." Sin (*khata*) in general means to miss or fall short of the mark (as an arrow or spear); transgression (*pesha*) means essentially a breach of trust or the fracturing of relationship; and iniquity (*avon*), to distort what is good—activity against right order and goodness. Interestingly in Ps 51 David also uses three distinct Hebrew words to illustrate God's capacity to deal with all our sin: David prays, "*Blot out* my transgressions . . . *wash me* of my iniquity . . . and *cleanse me* from my sin." We are shown in the old covenant that, yes, God had made a way to deal with iniquity, transgression, and sin—it is, for the moment "covered"—but not yet borne away to a place where God discards it eternally. Rather, it is said to be covered (e.g., Ps 85:2). Hebrews 10:4 informs us, "For it is not possible that the blood of bulls and goats could *take away* sins." The taking away had to await that ultimate sacrifice, as the writer explains just a bit later, "By that will we have been sanctified through the offering of the body of Jesus Christ once for all. And every priest stands ministering daily and offering repeatedly the same sacrifices, which can never *take away* sins. But this Man, after He had offered one sacrifice for sins forever, sat down at the right hand of God" (Heb 10:10–12).

So, a people arising from Abraham were chosen to represent the righteousness of God in the earth; a people who lived according to the righteous requirements of Yahweh, to demonstrate in the earth life under his government—government that delivered prosperity and fruitfulness. However, the terms of his government—the rules under which his favor would flow to them, had to be signposted (as the speed signs on the highway), at the very least so that ignorance could not be pleaded.

What he preferred was a people living that way without the necessity to signpost it as dramatically as it was at Sinai. He always desired that it be in their hearts by faith, and there strongly enough to govern both desire and resulting behavior. Ironically, right there at Sinai, Aaron and the others had convincingly demonstrated how essential the signposts were as they constructed and gave homage to their alternative calf. This was far, far short of the Abrahamic exemplification of "the way" preferred by Yahweh. Why, even Abraham's father had started out well but had then begun to worship strange gods! It seems that few there were who could walk in the way simply by and in faith. And so, temporarily, the legislation came in to govern that part of the time line that led up to Mashiach Yeshua's arrival and work—after which the Holy Spirit would replace Mashiach's limited earthly presence—and he would write the desire to please the Father upon each willing heart!

CHAPTER 5

The Wandering Jew

(Or, A Disobedient and Contrary People)

THE ENORMOUS SAGA THAT unfolds through God's choice of Moses and the deliverance of the Hebrew people from Egypt, followed by their wilderness wandering, is of far-reaching spiritual significance. A significance that spans all eras of time and people. For it is God's "object lesson" par excellence, demonstrating many spiritual truths and principles. It demonstrates that God cares, hears, and answers to deliver us from the captivities of darkness and oppression; it demonstrates that he gives opportunity to all, including the "pharaohs" of this world, to repent and cooperate with his plans; that the way out involves blood—that of a lamb—and requires obedience and faith; that the darkness of Egypt will not let go easily and will pursue us until it is buried in the "sea" of baptism. Many more lessons could be enumerated, but Israel's sojourn after the Red Sea is also instructive, because her failure to enter the fullness of what God had for her can be likened in some respects to her current situation.

Under Moses, and after such a mighty deliverance, the people refused to enter the land. Then, under Joshua, or Yeshua—that's right—the same name as our Savior and, indeed, meaning "savior" or "deliverer," faith rises, and they enter. The implication is that the law (Moses) was not able to bring them in, nor can it today. They will enter only with Yeshua and by faith in him.

Today they are again in a wilderness—they are in "desolation" (*eremos*) until the fullness of the gentiles is complete. Does that mean they are excluded until then? Or rejected entirely? Not at all—and Paul's purpose is to demonstrate this by pointing to himself as the example and archetype. God saved him. He was neither excluded nor rejected: he is "in," and so can be every Jew who will trust Jesus Christ for salvation.

Today, immediately, in the true Yeshua of whom Joshua is the type, any Jew may enter his or her salvation! For many however, God is still waiting for the turning, as he said through Isaiah (65:2) and as quoted by Paul in Rom 10:21:

> All day long I have held out my hands to a disobedient and contrary people.

CHAPTER 6

What the Prophets Saw

ANY BELIEVER WHO READS the Scriptures and hears today's multiplied end-times teachings will have pondered some of the prophetic writings of Ezekiel, Daniel, Isaiah, Micah, Zechariah, et al.

Among others, a potentially puzzling portion is the last chapters of Zechariah, which clearly use the terms "latter days" and "the day of the Lord" in a way that suggests far more than just the upcoming and immediate trajectory of Israel. And the picture Zechariah presents of these latter days by the Spirit of Yahweh is one that has some surprises, for we see nothing less than what appears to be a revival of the temple cult and restored worship in Jerusalem—and even sacrifice.

Can it be so?

In chs. 12 and 13, Zechariah speaks first, not of what had become known as *the* day of the Lord, but of a day of turning and a time of mourning and of salvation for Judah and the inhabitants of Jerusalem. To which every praying Christian shouts a resounding "Amen . . . let it be, Lord."

Zechariah, like Ezekiel, speaks of "living water" flowing from Jerusalem, wealth of nations coming to her—and, astonishingly, of the nations coming to her to celebrate the Feast of Tabernacles! Not only that, but every common thing in Jerusalem becoming sanctified and people again making sacrifice.

That God chose a particular place that had been recognized first as Salem, then Jebus and then the city of David and finally Jerusalem, is beyond question, as outlined in chapter 3. The site was anchored to the location of Gihon Spring, the karst-type spring whose name means "gushing forth." As previously discussed, this site had been recognized from the days of Abraham or even earlier as HaMakom—the Site or the Place.[1] Its significance lies in the fact that it was *chosen*—chosen as the location around which God's extraordinary plan of redemption was to unfold. Gihon quite clearly provides the "type" for the living water of which Jesus was later to speak, which he said would also be "springing [gushing] up" from within those who believed (John 4:14)—and its stream features in the prophets as well as in the Revelation of John. For example, Isaiah speaks of the people rejecting the waters of Shiloah, which flow softly (Isa 8:6),[2] for which rejection he would bring over them the waters of "the" river (the Euphrates, representing the Assyrians). As the Euphrates represented the prideful might of the Assyrians, Gihon represented the quiet and peaceful blessing of God on his people. Babylon had the Euphrates, and Nineveh boasted the Tigris. What did Jerusalem have? Certainly not that kind of river, but she did have something of greater and deeper significance. The psalmist said, "There *is* a river whose streams make glad the city of God, the holy place of the tabernacle of the Most High" (Ps 46:4), and Gihon was that stream. In Isaiah's time King Hezekiah's engineers built the quite extraordinary tunnel system that directed (or "sent") the water from Gihon flowing beneath the city, to the pool known as Shiloah or Siloam (which means "sent"). These are the softly flowing waters of which Isaiah spoke. He said that because God's people had rejected what those waters represented, the "flood" of the Assyrian army would sweep over them, reaching

1. See Heard, *Temple Quest*; Heard, *Place*. In the author's view HaMakom was also Eden's site.

2. Shiloah described the Gihon Spring water system that flowed into Siloam.

the "neck"—a possible reference to the neck of land, the ridge of Moriah, which had also been known of old as Luz (or neck bone).[3]

Gihon was the spot, the sacred spot, where David had erected a temporary tent to house the ark of the covenant and other sacred objects. Why? Because he knew that *x* marked the spot for the later erection of the temple.

Both Isaiah and Micah made this identical statement about the "latter days": "Many people shall come and say, 'Come, and let us go up to the mountain of the LORD, to *the Bethel of Jacob*; He will teach us His ways, and we shall walk in His paths.' For out of Zion shall go forth the law, and the word of the LORD from Jerusalem" (Isa 2:3; Mic 4:2). Note that "the Bethel of Jacob" means that site Jacob named following his dream, when he said, "This is none other than Beyt-El [house of El] and the gateway of heaven" (see Gen 28:17). The Hebrew in the Isaiah and Micah passages literally says, "To the Bethel" or "To the house of God *of* Jacob" and *not* "To the house of *the* God of Jacob."

Some Christians take these prophetic statements from Isaiah and Micah to point to an expected earthly "millennial kingdom" under the rulership of Jesus Christ—and this may well be the case. Whatever position we take on that matter, the suggestion of sacrifice possibly being offered again in Jerusalem in latter days, to some extent, mystifies us all.

Yet, I believe there is an explanation in the fusion that I propose, as you will see as we proceed. But, before we come to that "fusion" there is quite a lot of ground that we need to cover . . .

---

3. Luz, meaning neck-bone. See https://en.wikipedia.org/wiki/Luz_(bone). It is possible that the southern ridge of Moriah, which is crescent shaped and appears to support the bulged head to its north, is the reason. A representation of this can be seen in FIG. 1 in the Appendix.

CHAPTER 7

Grace over against Grace!

WE ARE STANDING IN a long, straight, and dark tunnel. We realize that we are standing somewhere near the middle of its length because we can see a minute speck of light at the end in each direction, far away. Suddenly the tunnel becomes illuminated along its entire length, and we realize that it is full of events, receding into the distance in either direction. We then see that where we stand, we are near a central, prominent event: it is a now-empty cruciform—which somehow draws attention, because it mysteriously and majestically assumes sovereignty over all other events—civilizations, empires, kings, and despots, in either direction. We recognize that we are positioned at history's deliberate and singular crux! The outstretched arms of the cruciform or cross seem to reach or certainly point, on the one hand, into the far past, and on the other, into the furthest future—as though to reconcile and join the one to the other.

How true it is that history has indeed a central event! Civilizations greater and lesser have come and gone; wars and seismic shifts of nations and states have made their marks along the line we call time; figures of note and significance have risen and faded, altering to one extent or another the trajectory of history. But one event and one only divides that time line into its most significant "before" and "after."

It is a single event yet comprised of three main components—an arrival, a death, a resurrection (complemented by an ascension). The three-in-one event has a unique symbol. It is the cross on which Jesus died, and it is the defining and central event of all of earth's history, because it was the most necessary, the most inevitable, and the most powerful! It is the ultimate demonstration of the grace of Yahweh Elohim to mankind; it is the symbol par excellence of that compelling grace which is always being extended to us.

How John Saw Things

We'll examine how John the apostle viewed it. He wrote something profound in these words: "And out of His *fullness* did we all receive, and *grace over-against grace*" (John 1:16 YLT). He used the Greek preposition *anti*, which we translate as "against" or "over against." Some translations have "upon," and the NIV has "in place of."

What does John mean?

The context makes his meaning clear for he explains in the next breath, "For the law was *given* through Moses, but grace and truth *came* through Jesus Christ" (John 1:17).

John is describing what came from the "fullness" of this Word-made-flesh Being. In 1:14, he makes this striking statement: "And we beheld His *glory*," and "glory" in both Hebrew and Greek means that which fills a thing; that of which it is comprised and which provides its substance. So that is why John then says, "And of His *fullness* have we received": and what we have received is . . . "*grace over against grace.*" This is the attribute that fills God. When Moses asked of God, "Show me your glory," Yahweh Elohim said, "I will make all my *goodness* pass before you" (see Exod 33:18–19). That is what God is full of!

The first manifestation of God's goodness and grace was *given*; the other *came*! Together they are described as grace over against grace, or one grace after another!

Can you see that John is saying that humankind has received two outstanding manifestations or expressions of God's extraordinary goodness? The first expression was "*given*," as John says, "*through* Moses"—through an intermediary. The second, however—the grace "over against" the first—*came!*

One *handed down*, the other *arriving*—among us. One given across a gap, the other bridging that gap!

The first expression was his kindness in providing the standard—the signposts, so that we knew what he is like and exactly what was expected of us. We are without excuse!

The second was him arriving! Arriving among us as fully human both to show us how to live and to meet in entirety and in himself all the requirements of those signposts. To meet them in our behalf—and then invite us *into* himself so that we become included in his success simply (though not necessarily always easily) by walking hand in hand and heart in heart with him!

Competing Covenants?

It is my view that too many Christians have tended to view the two great covenants as competing rather than as complementary; for them, there is law and there is grace—appearing (or made to appear) as competing opposites.

In such a view, there is no grace or goodness in the law. It's as though God started being gracious at a particular point in what we know as time. As if to parody this there are even some who seem to feel that the God of the old covenant is quite different to that portrayed in the new; or as though God used to be always severe and angry, but somehow "got up one morning" with a change of heart and decided to be nice to us!

And it is true that the coming of Jesus, followed by the sending of his Spirit, has effected something that the law with its high demands and inability to provide enabling could not do. But we have seen that there certainly was reward—and the Spirit was not inactive or absent in the old order. For people recognized him and his work—and it was not just the prophets but men like Nehemiah and David and others.

Any tendency for Christians to discard or neglect the Old Testament as though not relevant to them should be of enormous concern, for we all must see that God has curated the experiences of his people through time, for our benefit. Yes, as Paul says, "For us on whom has come the end of the ages" (1 Cor 10:11).

In that same passage he twice reminded us that what occurred with the people of God in the old covenant has all been written down specifically for our benefit, as examples and as admonition for us on this side of Calvary.

We must think about the special realm God created for us: we were created as creatures analogous to him, to live within a specially created realm known as time. He, living in timelessness (otherwise known as eternity), made this special linear realm, having a beginning, a middle—and an end. He made it for us! Eternity is nothing like this realm of ours. We humans are inclined to picture eternity as a very, very loooong time, but—it is not time at all! Though difficult, we must try to rid ourselves of "time" thinking if we are to have any idea of God's realm.[1] But, having said that, here we are, bounded by and within *time*. It is linear—a long line, which had a beginning and will, almost certainly, have an end—that is, time will become unnecessary and will be discarded.[2] Jesus said that he is the Alpha and the Omega, the Beginning and the End. He began this time realm, and he will end it!

The Apogee

As we look at this linearity, the time line we call history (the tunnel in the illustration above) as having a beginning and an end, we also see that it has a central event: the event that establishes the most significant "before" and "after." Of course, any event along the line has, necessarily, a before and an after, but there is one event that is the most important event in all history. It is the one that defines

---

1. See Ian Heard, *The Person: I, Wisdom (God in the Time Realm)* (Eugene, OR: Resource, 2019).

2. When the KJV translates Rev 10:6, "that there should be time no longer," it is not referring to an end to time as we experience it but to no more delay. However, in the author's view, since time is a construct made for humanity and creation, it will be discarded when this creation is discarded.

history! Its before and after—and how we relate to them, in fact—also defines who we are!

The event I speak of, the apogee of history as we have seen, is, of course, Calvary, with its necessary birth, life, death, resurrection, and ascension of the God-Man, Jesus Christ, for the redemption of a desperately vitiated humankind. And, not only does it divide history—it also divides those who recognize their need of redemption from those who compound their felony of unbelief by refusing to acknowledge their need.

Since *the* event had to occur at a point along the line we call time, everything prior to it and subsequent to Adam's fall necessarily *pointed ahead* to it. Everything since that central event both issues from it and points back to it.

We have need to see therefore that human history beyond Adam is essentially constituted of a huge, single redemption event! Or, to say it another way, this is the main event!

What this means is that old covenant and new covenant should not be treated as so many seem to, as polarized or competing dispensations, but rather as the perfectly complementary and unified prologue and epilogue that they are. They constitute a whole; a whole manifestation of both the grace and the mercy of our wonderful God! And must be treated thus. As has so aptly been said a long time before me, "The New is in the Old, concealed; the Old is in the New, revealed."

For Christians to greatly impoverish themselves by treating with disdain or even as irrelevant what God has curated for our admonition, understanding, and learning of his ways—and how to walk in them—is to treat God with disdain. For he and his word are one. His program and plan are one.

It is grace *all the way*!

Permit another illustration: A sundial works on the principle of creating a shadow answering the movement of the Sun across our globe as the Earth rotates, ninety-three million miles from it. The sundial consists of a flat, calibrated face on which is positioned a triangular post or pillar called a gnomon, with an edge (known as the style) facing the Sun. If we look at the procession of history as being like the procession of the shadow across the face of the sundial, Jesus Christ on a cross is the gnomon. He and Calvary stand as the central event of earth's history. It is his shadow and that of the central event of Calvary that defined the very beginning of history's "day" and have tracked across the face of Earth's time-dial all the way to our day and beyond. The shadow is created by the cross, behind which is the light of God's face—and the shadow does not lie. Earth's time is determined in relation to that event, whether we see it or not.

Calvary was high noon, the critical moment of earth's history when the shadow moved from morning to afternoon. On this side, the shadow now lengthens and before long will be extinguished by the night.

CHAPTER 8

A Joined People

ON EITHER HISTORIC SIDE of this central, grand, and unifying event—that of God's grace arriving and being exhibited on earth in the person of God—are the people who have feared him and who follow him.

Salvation for every one of them is in that central event spoken of and illustrated in the previous chapter. To further expand on that . . .

Yes, those who lived before Calvary as well as we who live after it are all saved *in* that event. For, you see, Calvary is, in fact, *the* event, which is above and unconstrained by time: Jesus Christ is "the Lamb slain *from* the foundation of the world" (Rev 13:8), and according to Peter, he was "foreordained *before* the foundation of the world" (1 Pet 1:20).

For those who feared God and lived in obedience to him in what we call the old covenant, salvation was just as much ultimately secured for them in Jesus Christ at Calvary as for those of us who live in this part of the time line. Their salvation was in *prospect* and ours in *post-spect*! The "above-time," history-embracing, and consuming event of Calvary occurred ahead for them and behind for us because, necessarily, we all live somewhere along the line.[1]

---

1. In this author's view, time is the construct ordained by God for this creature's temporary habitation and journey. See Heard, *Person*.

Calvary stretches back and embraces its past through and in every sacrifice the priests made at the tabernacle and the temple. In them all, Jesus is being described as "the Lamb slain from the foundation of the world."

It stretches forward to embrace all on this side of it: it is, as we said, *the* defining event of the time line we call history.

Every sacrifice of those far-off days represented and pointed to the fulfilling and supremely efficacious sacrificial Lamb who was coming; and each of those forward-pointing offerings temporarily "covered"[2] the sin and guilt of the sacrificer until all offerings were consummated in the offering that summed them all up—brought them all together as one, no longer only to cover but to "take away" sin and guilt. This is made ever so clear in Heb 10, where the writer reiterates several times that the blood of those sacrifices could never "take away" sins; however, the new and living way, in contrast, clearly does so. This makes clear that the temporary covering over in the Old simply awaited final removal by and with that consummating sacrifice of Jesus Christ.

It is of extraordinary significance that the greatest and last of the prophets of the Old cried out, when he saw Jesus approaching, those powerful words that somehow join the two together and make the time line indivisible, "Behold the Lamb of God who *takes away* the sins of the world!" (John 1:29; cf. 1:36).

Calvary Joins!

Seeing history in this way unites the people of God throughout time. The joining event, the coupling link, is Calvary. Before and after become one, in, at, and because of Calvary. It is true that living on the other side—the prior side—may have been more onerous and difficult—with, for example, the awful toll on animal life being horrendous; but it speaks. Indeed, it *shouts*—of both the cost and the seriousness of *sin*! Our unbelief and insistence on self-government arising therefrom is no trifling matter as so many in

---

2. See Ps 32:1, for example. In Lev 4:20 sin is "atoned for." The Hebrew word *kaphar* means to cover.

our day customarily treat it. It must be seen as that impenetrable dark wall that separates humankind utterly from the presence and holiness of God. Likewise, the horrendous Lamb-of-God sacrifice that consummated them all must be seen for what it is!

It is this matter of us being united that is essentially the subject of this book, for if Calvary unites, its unifying purpose and effect may perhaps be deeper and wider than we think. For if every sacrifice leading up to it represents it and, to some degree, becomes part of it (because it consummates them), is it possible that among those people known as Jews who have not comprehended or received the significance of Yeshua Mashiach, there will come a new recognition and joining of the two in our time—or later? I must ask you to bear with me here, for I am not speaking of a reliance on the old system as efficacious. I am speaking, rather, of a time when the full and extraordinary richness in the symbolism and meaning of the old covenant becomes newly recognized and embraced by those within the new covenant. (This, at a time when some in the church have succumbed to criticisms coming from the world of strident "new" atheists and God haters. We hear a growing number of pastors and teachers who attempt to diminish and "talk down" the Old Testament as flawed and not a true picture of the Christian God. They do not see that they are in grave danger of white-anting the foundation on which redemption history stands.)

As I said, I am speaking also of a time and a hope in which the total efficacy of Calvary as the consummation of everything in the Old becomes newly comprehended by many who have been clinging to the Old—albeit at this time in their history, not dependent on the shedding of blood.

For if the types and their reality become joined, is not the whole greater than either?

Let me provide an example. In 1 Cor 10, Paul quite unequivocally sees (and places together) the twin baptisms of Israel (within the sea and within the cloud) as the events that joined them irrevocably to Moses (their Christ-type), in just the same way as the Christian is joined to Christ in baptism in both water and the Holy Spirit! Paul effectively makes us one and the same people; the first, experiencing Jesus Christ in prospect, the other (us), in post-spect. More than that, he writes that they of the Old participated *in Christ* as their spiritual food and drink, in the manna and with the water from the rock (which, he said, "was Christ"!).

As for them, so for us in the New—he is both our food and drink (John 6:51; 4:13). Here is the passage:

> Moreover brethren, I do not want you to be unaware that all our fathers were under the cloud, all passed through the sea, all were *baptized into Moses in the cloud and in the sea*, all ate the same spiritual food, and all drank the same spiritual drink. For they drank of that spiritual Rock that followed them, and that Rock was Christ. (1 Cor 10:1–5)

As we have said, the life of Christ, his defining purpose and his life's defining event—Calvary, stands above all history and spans history as nothing else does. It gathers history together, making it a unity and making the people who follow him, both before and after that event, one.

Therefore it should not surprise us if a day comes when the meaning of the sacrificial system of the Old, in the fullest way possible, comes crashing into the spiritual consciousness of Christians; and, on the other hand, when the fullest meaning of Calvary, reflecting and completing all that the Old meant, likewise dawns with a crash into the spiritual consciousness of Jews who are seeking truth about Mashiach. I for one pray it is so!

Remember, we are using Saul of Tarsus as our archetype!

CHAPTER 9

"On Me . . . Whom They Pierced"

(Zech 12:10)

IN A BREATHTAKING TELESCOPIC VIEW, the prophet Zechariah speaks of the extraordinary events destined to come to pass for the city of God and her people as we draw closer to the conclusion of things in our limited time realm (as discussed in the previous chapter). Although the view through the telescopic lens is foreshortened so that distant landscapes are pulled in close, making them somewhat difficult to distinguish and interpret, Zechariah is able to highlight for us the essential elements.

Here are some of those primary elements characterized in chs. 12–14:

- Jerusalem is to cause confusion and disarray and will become like a stone that damages those who abuse her. Those who come against her will be burned and destroyed while she is established and strong (12:2–9).

- There will be a supernatural work of grace and a recognition among her people of their true and only Mashiach. Their eyes will be opened to "see" him whom they have pierced. Some translations have here in v. 10 "look unto," and the Hebrew can certainly mean that as well as "consider." It certainly appears that a very significant season of recognition is coming for the Jewish people. We must pray so!

- It will be a season of turning away from idolatrous pursuits and false foretellings and speculations about Mashiach, and there will be a refining work of grace among them so that a purified remnant is seen.

- There will be a final effort against her, but the Lord's presence will be tangible—his feet, as it were, standing on the Mount of Olives, both defending his own and making a way of escape amidst great upheaval (14:1–9)! The living water, always symbolized by Gihon Spring, will again flow, representing the presence of God.

- Jerusalem will not only be rescued but raised up again in greatness and inhabited while retribution plays out on those who have abused her and her Lord (14:10–15).

- Finally, the once-thought-improbable fusion, which is the thesis of this book, is seen, as Jewish people together with people from the nations join together in glorious worship of true Mashiach.

In a moment we will consider the unfolding of this fusion, which begins here with these extraordinary and world-changing events of which Zechariah enthuses.

CHAPTER 10

"All Things Together in Christ"
(Eph 1:10)

ZECHARIAH SPEAKS FROM THE other side of Calvary—but into this side. He had seen what God sees and had been pleased to divulge to him. It is, in my view, similar to what Paul saw about all things being brought together in Christ. Old and New are reconciled and at last seen to be more unified than we had dared to contemplate. Old and New are not as polarized or opposed as we had thought, for they are indeed all of a whole, in Jesus Christ—Mashiach!

It is the most significant and telling events of what Zechariah and other prophets call "the day of the Lord" to which I now call your attention.

In doing so, let's first understand a few things about this "day" . . .

It necessarily comes at the end—as the consummation. The prophets use the term in the same way as we do today when we say things like "he has had his day" or "her day will come." This is the day that arrives after everyone else has had theirs; the soothsayers, the prognosticators and speculators, the despots, the dictators; all the prideful and the boasting. All those who thought they could build a kingdom that would last, or a tower that would reach to the heavens—all the kings, captains, and mighty men of whom the

Revelation of John speaks in 19:8! When they have all had their say and had their day and exhausted their vanities . . . it is then the day of the "rider on the white horse" of Rev 19:11 (note: not the one of human pretense of Rev 6:2).[1]

Yes, after all that and all those comes—the day of the Lord! It is the season of consummating events that draw history and our human time line to its magnificent conclusion!

And behold! What do we see in that time? A phenomenon we would not have guessed at—would not have conceived possible. Yet here it is in black letters on white pages; history before it happens, given in the providence of God through the mouth of this man, this prophet, Zechariah.

What he sees is miraculous, for it is, I believe, a fusion. For here is, as God always intended, Jerusalem once more the center of God's plan and of the culminating events for planet Earth! In my view, it is exactly where the story, the time line of man, all began. Furthermore, as the place where the final beautiful fusion of Old and New occurs.

And now—some important understandings concerning the city and the people, the Jews . . . *and*, this coming fusion.

The City of the Great King!

Jerusalem stands as the epicenter of God's earthly program. Always has been; always will be while Earth remains. The Bible makes this clear. On both sides of Calvary, all nations and peoples have great relevance and significance, but they prosper or languish, rise or fall, in relation to Israel and her representative city, Jerusalem—and in accord with their treatment of her. Jesus himself called Jerusalem "the city of the great king" (Matt 5:35), and we see in Zech 14:16 that they will come to worship her *King*—as also in Zech 9:9 (more on this below):

1. In this author's view, the white horse rider of Rev 6:2 is prideful humankind and his belief in self-salvation. See Ian Heard, *Windows on a World Gone Wrong: The Revelation of John in Fresh and Refreshing New Light* (Maitland, FL: Xulon, 2001).

Rejoice greatly, O daughter of Zion!
Shout, O daughter of Jerusalem!
Behold, your *King* is coming to you;
He is just and having salvation,
Lowly and riding on a donkey,
A colt, the foal of a donkey.

Through the time line of our history, two cities have represented and contrasted human plans and self-effort, over against God's plan and work. The two are Babylon and Jerusalem: one is corrupt and destined for destruction, and the other is strategic in the fulfillment of God's purpose on earth until its end—and then, in the new earth, the new Jerusalem also appears to be strategic as the dwelling of God with us.

It is true that Christian believers on earth belong spiritually now to "the Jerusalem that is above," as Paul explains in Gal 4, and that the earthly, physical Jerusalem is currently "in slavery with her children" (v. 25). In another of God's mysteries, the "Jerusalem above," the "new" Jerusalem, will "come down" to replace the old—but it will keep its name.

Replacement Theology?

While true that God's presence in the earth is now particularly within Christ's body, the church, and she is his earthly temple (as are its individuals), she has *not* replaced Israel or Jerusalem. There is no "replacement theology" in the Bible! While there is to be a "new Jerusalem," up until that time, God's plans still include Israel and earthly Jerusalem. Why on earth would Jesus say, "I'll be back," and make this the place of his return, if it was all over for them?

He said to the people of Jerusalem, as above, that they would be desolate and abandoned until . . . "*until* you say, 'Blessed is he who comes in the name of the Lord'" (Matt 23:39). Now, they had already said that, just a few days before, as Jesus had ridden into the city (Matt 21:9). That had been their shout then, so it is telling that Jesus used their very own words back to them, now that their mood had diametrically changed. Ellicott in his commentary on this passage says this, "There is obviously a reference to the fact that the words quoted from Ps 118:26 had been uttered by the crowd but a few days before on His solemn entry into Jerusalem. Not till those words should be uttered once again—not in a momentary burst of excitement, not with feigned Hosannas, but in spirit and in truth—would they look on Him as they looked now."[2]

At that return to the "city of the great king" they would, as Zechariah had so presciently said, look on *"me whom they pierced"* (Zech 13:10).

Yes, the king will return to his age-old city: that center which arose around the Gihon Spring, the gushing spring that had always been the "type" of living water flowing at and from the earthly throne of the King.

*"The Word of the Lord—*from *Jerusalem"*

Isaiah's words about this "day," the last day, are quite extraordinary. Both he and Micah call our attention to the site that Jacob had called Bethel (house of God) (Isa 2:3; Mic 4:2). Now both these prophets cite it as "the Beyt-El [Bethel] *of* Yaakov [Jacob]" . . . which translates simply as "the house of God *of* Jacob" and not "the house of *the* God of Jacob." It is without the definite article before "God."[4] The Bethel of Jacob was where he had his dream of the heavenly staircase and angelic beings. That location was known to the patriarchs as HaMakom, the Place, and throughout antiquity, as the site of the Gihon Spring. It was on the southern ridge of Mount Moriah. It was the site whence Melchizedek, king of Salem, "brought out," as Gen 14:18 tells us, bread and wine for Abram.

---

2. "Matthew 23:39," in *A Bible Commentary for English Readers by Various Writers*, edited by Charles John Ellicott (London: Cassell and Co., 1905; (https://biblehub.com/commentaries/ellicott/matthew/23.htm).

3. In full, Zech 12:10 says, "And I will pour on the house of David and on the inhabitants of Jerusalem the Spirit of grace and supplication; then they will look on Me whom they pierced. Yes, they will mourn for Him as one mourns for *his* only *son and* grieve for Him as one grieves for a firstborn."

4. See ch. 6.

It was later the water supply for the Jebusite stronghold (Jebus) which was to become the city of David—and Zion.

This was always the true and original Beyt-El or Bethel and where Jerusalem and the temple were to become established.[5]

It is *from* here, say both Isaiah and Micah, that in that day, the word of the Lord will sound out! Here are those words:

> Many nations shall come and say,
> "Come, and let us go up to the mountain of the Lord,
> To *the Bethel of Jacob;*
> He will teach us His ways, and we shall walk in His paths."
> For *out of Zion* the law shall go forth,
> And the word of the Lord *from Jerusalem.* (Isa 2:2–3; cf. Mic 4:1–2)

What Satan Hates

It is very clear in our day that there are two groups around whom Satan's destructive energies center. Satan is, first and foremost, the enemy of the church, which he hates with unmitigated and unrelenting venom. As the bride of Christ, the church will soon occupy a place above the one he so irrevocably relinquished, in the presence of the Almighty! More than that, she is the regent of Jesus Christ in the earth, standing in the power and authority bequeathed to her by her Lord—authority to demolish strongholds established by Satan in lives and systems and hearts (2 Cor 10:3–5). Satan is aware of the purposes of God only inasmuch as they are disclosed in God's word . . . beyond that he knows little. But there is enough there for him to be bitterly opposed, not only to the church but also to the Jewish people for they, too, feature prominently and with a future in that word. In my view it appears to be, for many of them, a future of glorious, redemptive fusion.

---

5. See Heard, *Temple Quest.*

Against One, Against All

Because Satan has taken the ridiculous and finally untenable position of opposition to the Almighty, he is opposed to all that emerges as part of God's purpose in time. Against God and therefore against all those included as his, and against all his plans. He is mostly reactive. He is proactive only insofar as the purposes of God have been disclosed and have an obvious trajectory. And that obvious trajectory is written, disclosed—and irrevocable! It includes a glorious bride, comprised of multitudes from both covenants. He sees it and knows that what is written, the trajectory and its conclusion, eternally excludes him and his angels. Nonetheless, in blindness and fury he nurtures the vain hope of maximizing damage to both the purpose and the people of God. The only "satisfaction" he can take with him to the eternal pit is that of destroying the faith of those he may have succeeded in turning to his folly.

There is clearly (and wonderfully) a sense in which Christian believers who trust God and walk in the Spirit certainly know more than the devil, for the Holy Spirit discloses truth to us that he cannot see. Indeed, Jesus stated this marvelous truth of the Holy Spirit:

> When He, the Spirit of truth, has come, He will guide you into all truth; for He will not speak on His own authority, but whatever He hears He will speak; and He will tell you things to come. (John 16:13)

That most certainly puts us way ahead of the Satan—as spiritually powerful as he may pretend to be, he has neither this nor the majestic authority of Jesus Christ, our Lord! We need *never* fear him! And . . . praise God for that truth!

God Is Jealous for His People

Of Israel God said, "He who touches you, touches the apple of my eye!" (Zech 2:8). God is sensitive about those who are his. To touch them maliciously is metaphorically to poke the pupil of God's eye!

Conversely, all who oppose God also oppose *all* his people, as indicated above. Anyone who has visited the land and the people of Israel will surely have sensed that there is an answer—especially for God-fearing Israel who, as Paul taught us, are temporarily blinded and set aside to facilitate a larger blessing: that of bringing in and grafting in the gentile world! I am speaking of a "fusion"—and the manner or mechanism by which Yeshua Mashiach becomes received as the pivot, the linchpin who, rather than keeping old and new divided, is the One in whom *all* become reconciled.

Also . . . consider the building of competing temples . . . that which God is building—where his Spirit now dwells, in the individuals who comprise the church—and that which the Jewish people will probably seek to build in the final days.

It is my view that parallel to the building of a physical temple and zeal among some Jews to restore it and even restore sacrifice, that at that time revelation will come to many seekers. What better time to have eyes opened to the truth that everything they seek to restore has already been fully accomplished—for them! What better moment for the "spirit of grace and supplication" prophesied by Zechariah to flood over them than when they are trying to reinstitute what has been so comprehensively sublimated through Yeshua Mashiach? There is already a steady and accelerating movement among Jewish people, including numbers of rabbis who are receiving, like Saul of Tarsus, a revelation of the fullness of truth as they hear the gospel! I believe this movement is gathering momentum, and as it does, *the fusion* has already begun. It is in embryo: the fusion that will change the spiritual climate of the worlds of Judaism and Christianity while ushering in a worldwide awakening. I believe this is why the preaching of the gospel to the Jewish people must be couched in terms of everything the Torah and prophets have said. Today, projects such as the Messianic Prophecy Bible project and the work of One for Israel, together with multiplying messianic Christian fellowships and intercessory groups in Israel, are the seedbed for this awakening.[6] These are people who are not shouting the gospel across a chasm but from

---

6. See https://free.messianicbible.com/; https://www.oneforisrael.org.

within the mindset of Jewish religious and secular cultures, under-standing, and Scriptures.

The Meaning and Importance of Elijah's Seven Thousand

In Rom 11, Paul uses the seven thousand who had not bowed the knee to Baal in the days of Elijah as an illustration of the true—and therefore whole and perfected—Israel. As I indicated in chapter 1, the number seven, particularly in contexts such as this, bibli-cally represents fullness or completeness as it certainly does in the Elijah episode. These, in Elijah's day, constituted those with whom God could work; these were his real Israel, true Israel. Those whose hearts were genuine. This genuineness is true of any group. There are those who are genuinely committed and those whose "belong-ing" and participation are ambivalent or equivocal. For the latter, it depends always on what's in it for them.

And so, says Paul, there will be a valid "Israel." These are those, as he explains in Rom 11:23 "who do not continue in unbe-lief." And so, to . . .

The Meaning of "All Israel" in Romans 11:26

Extending the point above further, we note that Paul has just spoken of the "*fullness* of the Gentiles" and now writes, "And so . . . *all* Israel will be saved." The word *so* here is the Greek οὕτως (*houtos*), meaning "in like manner," and it appears that Paul is say-ing that just as there is a fullness of the gentiles, just so—or in like manner—there is also to be a fullness or an "all" of Israel! Indeed, several good translations write "and *in this way* all Israel will be saved."[7] As above, the "all" is the completeness represented by the seven thousand in Elijah's day, whom God saw as truly his. Not all gentiles will be saved, but there will be a fullness of them—and not all Jews will be saved, but there will be a fullness of them. In fact, in

---

7. See, for example, NIV, Holman, CEV, CSB, and others.

Rom 11:12, Paul has already said this about his own people: "Now if their fall is riches for the world, and their failure riches for the Gentiles, how much more their *fullness!*"

We must remember that Jesus alluded to the total plan when he said this: "And *other sheep* I have which are not of *this* fold; them also I must bring, and they will hear my voice; and there will be *one flock* and *one shepherd*" (John 10:16).

We should also note that for devout Jewish people, their "shepherd" is still Moses . . . but according to these words of Jesus, he will become their Shepherd. That "one flock and one shepherd" of which he spoke is of telling significance and can be compared with Paul's remarkable words in Eph 2:14–17 here:

> For He Himself is our peace, who *has made both one*, and has broken down the middle wall of separation, having abolished in His flesh the enmity, that is, the law of commandments contained in ordinances, so as *to create in Himself one new man* from the two, thus making peace, and that He might reconcile them *both* to God in one body through the cross, thereby putting to death the enmity. And He came and preached peace to you who were afar off and to those who were near.
>
> For through Him we *both* have access by one Spirit to the Father.

When Paul uses that Greek word εἰρήνη (*eirene*), meaning peace (used three times in three verses), we must be aware that it carries all the meaning of its Hebrew counterpart *shalom*—welfare, wholeness, and completeness. Here is the note from a Greek lexicon to help us:

> *eirếnē* (from *eirō*, "to *join, tie together* into *a whole*")— properly, *wholeness*, i.e. when all essential parts are joined together; *peace* (God's gift of *wholeness*)[8]

Paul's meaning is that in the One known as Peace, gentiles and Jews have been joined as a whole—a radical concept for both

---

8. "HELPS Word-Studies," in "1515. eiréné," Bible Hub, 2021 (https://biblehub.com/greek/1515.htm); emphases original.

parties. In my view, we have all been made, in him, true Jews (and hence, "all Israel"). We see the same idea in Gal 3:28, which is, unfortunately, contentious—yet nonetheless true, I believe. Here it is:

> There is neither Jew nor Greek, there is neither slave nor free, there is neither male nor female; for you are all one in Christ Jesus.

Just as gentile and Jew have been "peaced" together to become a true and whole "Israel," Gal 3:28 should be read, I believe, to mean that *in* him, there is now neither Jew nor Greek—*only Jew*; now neither slave nor free—*only free*; now neither male nor female—*only male*. Jesus Christ is the *one and only* true, free, male Jew—and we have *all* been brought *into him*! The context of Gal 3 is not ministry; it is inheritance. In the old covenant only a free, male Jew could inherit, but in Jesus we have now all been qualified to inherit.

It is thus, therefore, that we *all* become . . .

Partakers of the Root and Richness

It is important for Christians to recognize that we have been *grafted into* something much bigger than individuals and much deeper than a novel or recent idea. We, on this side of Calvary, have been joined to something that is God's big idea! This joining or grafting in is with the profound purpose that we bear fruit as the product of the whole tree. People today are seeking their roots and ancestry as never before. There is a yearning for attachment and depth. Paul reminds us here that what the Christian believer has been grafted into goes back to Abraham and before. It is stock of extraordinarily rich pedigree! And, so that we may be grafted like branches from a wild olive into this beautifully cultivated tree of such breeding, some have been broken off to facilitate our participation. As we've seen, it is participation in the big thing, the scheme, the program of *fusion* that predates Abraham. It is into *the* people—the sons of God (the benei Elohim).[9] A branch grafted into a tree becomes

9. See Ian Heard, *The People: The Sons of God (through the Eyes of a*

as much a part of that tree as any other part. When the graft has taken, the tree then is not a tree plus something else—it is *the* tree! We have been made one; we have been "peaced."

It was unbelief that caused some of them to be broken off to make way for us to become partakers of the rich juice and sap from the root.[10] Too many Christians choose to ignore what is available to them from those roots and the sap to their serious detriment. It is whence their spiritual DNA is derived. It is their pedigree.

Isaiah informs us about this Root. He reveals that the ancient Root materializes and becomes defined and consummated in a Person who is its demonstration in the flesh. The line, the pedigree, the long breeding are brought to fullest revelation in . . . him!

Here is a portion of Isa 11 from the Berean Standard Bible:

> Then a shoot will spring up from the stump of Jesse, and a
> Branch from his roots will bear fruit.
> The Spirit of the LORD will rest on Him—the Spirit of wis-
> dom and understanding,
> the Spirit of counsel and strength, the Spirit of knowledge
> and fear of the LORD.
> And He will delight in the fear of the LORD.
> He will not judge by what His eyes see, and He will not
> decide by what His ears hear,
> But with righteousness He will judge the poor, and with
> equity He will decide for
> the lowly of the earth.
> He will strike the earth with the rod of His mouth and slay
> the wicked with the breath of His lips.
> Righteousness will be the belt around His hips, and faithful-
> ness the sash around His waist. (Isa 11:1–5 BSB)

> On that day the Root of Jesse will stand as a banner for
> the peoples. The nations will seek Him, and His place of
> rest will be glorious. On that day the Lord will extend
> His hand a second time to recover the remnant of His
> people from Assyria, from Egypt, from Pathros, from

Watcher) (Eugene, OR: Resource, 2018).

10. See Rom 11:17–20.

Cush, from Elam, from Shinar, from Hamath, and from
the islands of the sea.

> He will raise a banner for the nations and gather the exiles
> of Israel;
> He will collect the scattered of Judah from the four corners
> of the earth.
> Then the jealousy of Ephraim will depart, and the adversar-
> ies of Judah will be cut off.
> Ephraim will no longer envy Judah, nor will Judah harass
> Ephraim. (Isa 11:10–13 BSB)

It is into this One that we are all invited. In being joined to
him, we are joined to the whole (for he *is* the Whole) to receive the
life arising from the entire root and stock!

How Can These Things Be?

It appears that Zech 12 with its poignant reference to a spirit of
grace and supplication being poured upon the house of David and
on the inhabitants of Jerusalem—and of them "looking on me
whom they have pierced"—predicts an extraordinary part of the
coming fusion.

Here it is in v. 10:

> And I will pour on the house of David and on the inhab-
> itants of Jerusalem the Spirit of grace and supplication;
> then they will look on Me whom they pierced. Yes, they
> will mourn for Him as one mourns for his only son, and
> grieve for Him as one grieves for a firstborn.

As I have mentioned, numbers of rabbis and other members
of the Hebrew community are experiencing epiphanies similar to,
if perhaps not always as dramatic as, that of Saul of Tarsus! The
ministry One for Israel (mentioned above) has many vital testi-
monies of such people. The groundswell has begun as a growing
number turn their eyes upon the pierced One and recognize in
him the coming together of all that the Torah and the prophets, the
festivals and the sacrifices were always pointing to!

Under the revelation of the Holy Spirit, the segue from one into the other is being seen not as any kind of betrayal of the one but as consummation and completion. And the recognition that when the requirements of the one have been fully met in a particular Person, no matter in which surprising or unexpected way, then, unless that Person is somehow a huge fraud—the new has surely arrived.

We are required to understand what a hurdle this can be for many Jewish individuals who may be inclined to pose legitimate questions, depending on their expectations and interpretations and those of their rabbis, such as "Where then is the peace Mashiach is supposed to bring to earth?"[11] It is true that the angelic host heralded his birth with the song "Glory to God in the highest, and on earth peace, goodwill toward men!" (Luke 2:14). And that, of course, is his desire and intent—but it comes with his government (or kingdom) to every heart that submits to it!

It seems to me to be exactly why epiphanous experiences are sometimes required.[12] It certainly was with Saul of Tarsus. And it also appears clear that God is going to act sovereignly. What he poured out upon Saul of Tarsus was just that: an outpouring of sovereign grace upon this man who was so vehemently, though ignorantly, raging against God. Saul's ignorance in that encounter is the key. As we've said, Saul was a zealot; he had, as he himself said, unrivalled zeal for the traditions of the fathers (Phil 3:6).

This is grace indeed! Grace that as Paul later said to the philosophers of Athens "winks at" or overlooks our ignorance (Acts 17:30).

11. A legitimate question. Jesus himself said, "I came not to bring peace but a sword." His peace is the product promised wherever his government (or kingdom rule) is freely received in hearts and lives (Rom 14:17).

12. It is worth noting that epiphanous revelation and appearances are not infrequent today among other seeking and searching zealots also, such as Muslims.

CHAPTER 11

Why the Feast of Tabernacles?

(Zech 14:16)

OF ALL THE JEWISH FEASTS, this was considered to be "the biggie"—the feast par excellence. It was the most popular as it was celebrated when the crops had been harvested and stored and the vintage completed.

But it was more than thanksgiving for all these things, for it looked back and it also looked forward: back to the vain wilderness wanderings when there were no crops or harvests and they lived in tents—and forward to God's great end-time harvest of ingathering foretold by Zechariah:

> And in that day, it shall be that living waters shall flow from Jerusalem,
> Half of them toward the eastern sea and half of them toward the western sea;
> In both summer and winter it shall occur.
> And the Lord shall be King over all the earth. In that day it shall be—
> "The Lord is one," and His name one. (Zech 14:8–9)

What Zechariah saw by the Spirit in this and other passages was people coming from all over the world—and especially those who have warred against Jerusalem—to worship God at the Feast of Tabernacles!

To say that this is remarkable is understatement indeed. But remarkable is what God does . . . and does so well!

Here is God's commandment to Moses for the Feast of Tabernacles, or *Sukkot*, as recorded in Lev 23:

> The Lord spoke to Moses, saying, "Speak to the children of Israel, saying: 'The fifteenth day of this seventh month shall be the Feast of Tabernacles for seven days to the Lord. On the first day there shall be a holy convocation. You shall do no customary work on it. For seven days you shall offer an offering made by fire to the Lord. On the eighth day you shall have a holy convocation, and you shall offer an offering made by fire to the Lord. It is a sacred assembly, and you shall do no customary work on it.
>
> 'These are the feasts of the Lord which you shall proclaim to be holy convocations, to offer an offering made by fire to the Lord, a burnt offering and a grain offering, a sacrifice and drink offerings, everything on its day—besides the Sabbaths of the Lord, besides your gifts, besides all your vows, and besides all your freewill offerings which you give to the Lord.
>
> 'Also, on the fifteenth day of the seventh month, when you have gathered in the fruit of the land, you shall keep the feast of the Lord for seven days; on the first day there shall be a sabbath-rest, and on the eighth day a sabbath-rest. And you shall take for yourselves on the first day the fruit of beautiful trees, branches of palm trees, the boughs of leafy trees, and willows of the brook; and you shall rejoice before the Lord your God for seven days. You shall keep it as a feast to the Lord for seven days in the year. It shall be a statute forever in your generations. You shall celebrate it in the seventh month. You shall dwell in booths for seven days. All who are native Israelites shall dwell in booths, that your generations may know that I made the children of Israel dwell in booths when I brought them out of the land of Egypt: I am the Lord your God.'"

And, here are some further facts about this feast in addition to its celebration and rejoicing over the harvest or ingathering:

- It was the seventh feast; it took place in the seventh month, and its duration was seven days. It speaks therefore of fulfillment and perfecting.
- It was *after* the Feast of Trumpets (which spoke of repentance) and Yom Kippur (of redemption).
- It featured (and still does) dwelling in temporary shelters as a reminder of Israel's wilderness sojourn. It signifies our earthly temporary sojourn and anticipation of our eternal dwelling.
- It was the feast to which foreign pilgrims also came.
- It included sacrifices.

As shown in chapter 5, the Jewish people are again in a "wilderness" experience, of which the first was a kind of "type"—a time of unbelief and temporariness, awaiting recognition of their Yeshua Deliverer to lead them in. How fitting therefore that the feast Zechariah speaks of in that "day" is Tabernacles!

An Ingathering

It appears that in this "day," there is to be a vast ingathering, a final recognition and embracing by Jew and gentile of repentance and of redemption as Light dawns.

This is what is most significant for us: The three major Jewish feasts were: Pesach or Passover, Shavuot (Pentecost), and Sukkot or Tabernacles. Since Passover and Pentecost have already seen their completion at Calvary and at the coming of Holy Spirit upon the church fifty days later, where then is the fulfillment of Tabernacles? Here it is, described by Zechariah as occurring in the endtimes. Its shadow or type remembered Israel's wilderness years and celebrated harvest in their new land. Now, in its fulfillment it will remember the years of being "set aside," as it were, in another wilderness until the fullness of the gentiles comes in—and then celebrates the joined ingathering! To which Christians today say, "Bring it on, Lord!"

If, as I propose, there is to be a beautiful fusion in which many Jews have a kind of epiphany of their true Mashiach as did Saul of Tarsus on the Damascus road—and at the same time many gentiles and Christians see the depth of meaning inherent in Judaism and the Jewish feasts, seasons, and rituals—then this feast is the one to express it. Why? Because it looks back to the wandering and then rejoices in the ingathering.

When Zechariah says that those who warred against Jerusalem will go up year after year to celebrate the Feast of Tabernacles, we need not see it as necessarily meaning every person, every year. Rather, that there will be a constant flow, over time, of those who once were enemies, recognizing truth and recognizing the One in whom it resides.

What an extraordinary and glorious celebration this may be: the consummation of the Jewish feast that best represents culmination and final ingathering of product. The feast that reminds of the years spent without harvest; the barren years of temporariness and sojourn while awaiting arrival at a place of fruitfulness and product; of eventual ingathering following repentance and ensuing redemption!

CHAPTER 12

The Fusion! A Scenario (Part 1)

WHILE VISITING ISRAEL IN LATE 2019 I witnessed a life-size re-production of the tabernacle set up by a Jewish hotelier on land next to his hotel, with a reenactment of the tabernacle ritual. That, along with a hologram display at Shiloh and other encounters, has contributed to my thinking and meditating on the supposal you are about to read.

In it I propose an imagined scenario for the season of which Zechariah speaks: a demonstration that assists Jew and gentile alike to see with clarity what has been fully accomplished through history and, in the future moment of which I speak, becoming recognized by searching Jew and gentile alike. Yes, recognized as completed in and by the Lamb of God who takes away the sin of the world!

Here it is . . .

We will suppose the year is, say, 2073. A beautiful new temple has been built in Jerusalem. Indeed, it has been erected, not on what had erroneously become known as Temple Mount but in its original, correct site in ancient Zion just above and to the west of Gihon Spring. Gihon, that age-old water source—and the reason why Salem, which became Jebus, then the city of David (or Zion; 2 Sam 5:7) and latterly Jerusalem, was located there. Gihon's flow has been mysteriously and indeed miraculously restored by seismic activity to something of its former glory and strength and now once more supplies water by its enormous force to the new temple's precinct. The name Gihon (or Gikhon) means "gushing forth" because of its ancient and most distinctive characteristic. It is what is known as a karst (or karstic) spring, capable of pushing its flow upward under pressure when constrained within piping.

The Jews have been restoring the temple cultus, and some sacrifices have already been offered. A high priest has been installed, and great excitement is abroad, gathering pace and intensity within devout Jewry. There is a groundswell of religious fervor, nationalism, and anticipation. Some motives are sound and good, others shadowy. For the devout, surely Mashiach's arrival is imminent, and once again, Israel will be the center of the work of God in the world!

Indeed, an arrival *was* at hand—but not quite as expected!

For in the days of which I write, the strangest of occurrences befell many, many of the Jews at that time, and especially those gathered in Jerusalem and nearby environs for the celebration of Sukkot. A great number of them had been "camping out" in their roughly assembled booths—especially the children, who always thought this feast the best of all!

All was excitement and incessant talk and festivity and to-do, with the men engaged in the serious man talk of politics and business and weather, and the women bustling and fussing about food or boasting of children's latest achievements. In the household into which we will intrude, the table, now set up in the booth or tabernacle wherein the children had spent the previous night, groaned under the blessings of the earth. The children's eyes ravished the stuffed peppers and fruits, the eggplants and cabbage, not to mention the potato knishes and pastries—and then there were the cinnamon-dusted tzimmes!

Suddenly then, in the midst of all this, something unexpected came.

It happened in this way; well, in this particular household and family this was how it occurred . . .

The father, Menachim, intoned a usual blessing over the evening meal, "Blessed are you, Lord our God, Ruler of the universe, at whose word all came to be . . . ," but no sooner had the words left his lips and the family had opened mouths to say the amein than Father was strangely overcome with a new and startling recognition: a revelation of what he had just said—and had so often said. Oh yes, in the past the words had come from sincerity, for Menachim was a good man who truly believed that the one called Ruler did indeed provide and bless. But today, why . . . today was different, for as he spoke that word "Ruler" there seemed to arrive, quite startlingly, not to his mind but to somewhere farther down and deeper in, these words that he knew to be from the prophet Micah:

> But you, Bethlehem-Ephrathah, though you are little
> among the thousands of Judah . . . out of you shall come
> forth to me The One to be *Ruler* in Israel, whose goings
> forth are from of old, from everlasting. (Mic 5:2)

So startling was it—and the way that it impinged on him deep within—that as everyone began to eat, Menachim could not. The words troubled him, and he was not sure why. At the insistence of his family, he almost reluctantly took food, but all knew something was amiss, and soon they began to ask.

"Father, this is not like you," said his favorite daughter, Esther, a svelte young woman with the most captivating green eyes, which shone from deep sockets above well-formed cheek bones and beneath dark brows, "Are you unwell?"

The whole family paused to hear.

"No, no," said Menachim, "Give me a moment or two to digest what has just come to me, and I will share it later," and with that the murmur and hum of converse gradually resumed, punctuated by the occasional outburst of hilarity and fun. Mother frequently cast an eye in Menachim's direction, but she knew and trusted him deeply and dearly enough to know that when he was ready, he would speak. And—she expected that what he had to say would be, as was usual, considered and wise.

When it came, it surprised even her.

The meal was done, and a relaxed contentment was upon the family. The beautiful autumnal day was fading, the temperature balmy and conducive to reverie, and the talk had drifted to "Remember the feast three years ago when Uncle Benyamin was still with us . . ." and similar fond reminiscences. It was then that Menachim spoke up.

"You all wondered what occurred as I prayed the blessing today," he began; "you will also remember the words of our great prophet Micah when he spoke of Bethlehem-Ephrathah as the place from which the One known to us as the Ruler, our long-expected Mashiach, would come?," the sentence ending with the uptick inflection of a question, to which most nodded recognition for they had been well schooled at synagogue.

Menachim continued, his measured tone and his carefully chosen words reassuring his hearers—who all trusted him, "It came to me, almost like an epiphany—like something I certainly did not expect, yet somehow dared not deny. It was so indelible. Do you know that the Christians' New Testament says—and history is clear that the one known as Yeshua of Nazareth, whom *they* call Mashiach, was indeed born there in Bethlehem-Ephrathah. But more than that: I also realized that Ephrathah of Bethlehem was the agricultural area associated with that town, and it was where the priests raised the special lambs for temple sacrifice. And when those lambs were born, they were swathed in bands and nurtured and kept ever so carefully so that none of their bones could be broken and they could be presented without spot or blemish! I saw this inwardly—like a picture—even as I prayed the blessing today . . ." Menachim paused and was almost overtaken again by the enormity and emotion of what had, with such undeniable certainty, come to him. The family, wide eyed, awaited his next words—and when they came, they too were rendered quite speechless because something of the enormity of what he was saying, and its ramifications, began to steal over them!

"I saw that the One of whom Micah spoke, and who is to be Ruler—the Eternal One—our awaited Mashiach, must surely indeed be the Mashiach of the Christian believers! He was born as predicted, right there in Ephrathah . . . the place of the sacrificial lamb! And then he was swathed in bands as the sacrificial lamb was swathed . . . it all came in upon me as though from Yahweh himself . . . I cannot explain it except to say I have never experienced such a sense of certainty. Why, as I recall, the one they called John the Baptist welcomed him as "the Lamb of God who takes away the sin of the world"! It is too coincidental to be any other. Too coincidental to expect it to occur again!"

The family was stunned, yet none could offer protest because as Menachim spoke another beautiful thing happened: they also, right down to the children, began also to see it—as though eyes were being opened, as though scales were falling off!

It was not only in the family of Menachim. No! All across the land known as Israel there were similar, though different, and unique events and occurrences. It was said that the one known as cohen or priest had entered the holy place where stood the altar of incense and the bread and the menorah and had experienced a light like that which Saul of Tarsus had experienced—and had emerged with shining face and in tears! In a synagogue, it was reported, a man had been reading the Haftarah portion from Zechariah (Zech 14:1–21) when the rabbi suddenly cried out that he had seen a vision of the living water flowing, indeed gushing out from Jerusalem—and that Yeshua was surely Mashiach who so clearly fulfills the symbols and types he had been reading about all his life! Apparently, it came to him in a flash of revelation as he was sincerely entering into the portion for that day!

Then also, among other prominent and respected rabbis and men of note the true Mashiach suddenly and sovereignly worked a work similar to that in Saul of Tarsus so long ago! In many different ways, similar events were occurring, and even protestors from dyed-in-the-wool traditionalists were hearing and understanding things to which they had been habitually closed minded! It was suddenly the talk of Jerusalem and Israel, and even more suddenly by social media networks it was spreading as a wildfire across the length and breadth of the land! And not only in Israel, but also immediately throughout sincere Jewry across the world, the reports began to appear, and it became evident that the ancient words of Zechariah were coming to pass before the eyes of an astonished world. It was suddenly this:

> And I will pour on the house of David and on the inhabitants of Jerusalem the Spirit of grace and supplication; then they will look on me whom they pierced. Yes, they will mourn for Him as one mourns for his only son and grieve for Him as one grieves for a firstborn. (Zech 12:10)

Yes, Yahweh Elohim was mysteriously and powerfully at work by the Spirit of his *khane* grace and entreaty! Prayer flowed freely as glorious recognition was being received and mercy entreated in what was indeed a sovereign outpouring. And the remarkable thing about it was its spontaneity and suddenness and wideness as well as the joyful, even impatient acquiescence and cooperation with which he was met! It was as though Jews from every nation as well as within Israel were now shouting, "Me too! Me too!" It is understatement indeed to say that the world had never seen anything like it—yet, naturally, skeptics and haters the world over mocked and lampooned and spun it every which way. But truth stands—and stood.

And so it was that there was a joyful joining of hearts of newly released and liberated-in-Christ Jewry and the Christian ecclesia, and the truth of Old and New began to be seen and experienced as a whole. And the whole began at last to become greater than the sum of its parts. Oh, and God began to raise up men and women of stature and wisdom to teach and prophesy, providing oversight and clarity—and who were able to say as Peter said of Pentecost's fulfillment, "This is *that* which was spoken." In his case, at Pentecost, it had been spoken by Joel, and now, in this time and this outpouring, by the prophets Micah and Zechariah and others.

But to return to our scenario . . .

"So," explained the traditionally clad high priest, who, having undergone a dramatic conversion experience to true Mashiach, now knew that he was called to walk his people through the story and through all that had been achieved at Calvary. Under his direction the temple ceremonies now became an object lesson that captivated Jewry and brought light and salvation to many. Too, Jews and gentiles, having heard of this extraordinary movement, had come from all over—to Jerusalem!

"Here is some blood from the killed lamb. I want you to picture that lamb as Yeshua Mashiach. The altar where it was killed has forever been replaced by his 'altar' at Calvary, not far from here. Do you see the sanctuary and that curtain at the rear of the holy place?"

We all nodded, and a few muttered yes.

"That place behind the curtain represents the holy of holies, the highest heaven where God, the Creator and Elohim, dwells. The Scriptures show us that when Mashiach died, he entered the presence of his Father with his own blood as the expiation for the sins of every one of us! He was representing every one of us as he fulfilled the words of our great prophet . . .

> Surely He has borne our griefs and carried our sorrows;
> Yet we esteemed Him stricken, smitten by God, and afflicted.
> But He was wounded for our transgressions,
> He was bruised for our iniquities;
> the chastisement for our peace was upon Him,
> and by His stripes we are healed.
> All we like sheep have gone astray;
> we have turned, every one, to his own way;
> and the Lord has laid on Him the iniquity of us all.
> (Isa 53:4–6)

"Do you see it? Open our darkened eyes now, O Great Lord."

And as he, clad with the priestly vestments—with the breast piece with the twelve stones and the ephod and the turban—continued, many among us began to weep. It was the arrival of the Spirit of grace and supplication among and upon us also, just as the prophet had foretold!

"I will carry now some blood of this lamb into the holiest place, and as I do, I ask you to picture—to see it only as a picture, an object lesson of what has already been completed. Yeshua taking his own blood into the most holy place into the presence of the Father. I am doing as he has done—but you will see that the curtain into the holiest is not now hiding it! For when he died and cried, 'It is finished,' that separating curtain was supernaturally rent in two. Indeed, I am inviting any upon whom recognition and acceptance is descending to come with me; to enter with me—for that is now where we are *all* invited!"

Some gasped. Others cried out or put hands over opened mouths or upon their heads. Tears flowed, and many began to move forward to enter in with the priest in a beautiful act of heart change and recognition.

And then the one dressed as high priest said,

"Since Mashiach was here with us, believers in him all over the world have reverently followed his instruction, remembering his sacrificial death by the taking of bread and wine together. We will do that together in a moment with all those to whom 'entering in' is being made real today. But, to bring clarity and full appreciation to our people Israel—to enable them to visualize and grasp the now-fulfilled meaning behind our ancient rituals—today we celebrate a revised form of our great and ancient Feast of Tabernacles. It is a practical demonstration of what Mashiach has done! This sacrifice and this blood represent the blood of Mashiach Yeshua, poured out on Calvary so long back, as fulfillment and completion of all the previous sacrifices of our old system, which was always pointing ahead to this."

Someone from the assembled gathering said, "But, if fulfilled then there is no need for more," to which the wise celebrant replied, "Quite so—and this is not more; oh no—it is simply for illustrative purposes, an object lesson with practical and visual demonstration so that our people can see what all the ritual and symbols of the Old were pointing to—and what actually occurred when our Mashiach was offered and how that offering has opened the curtain and made us one with Elohim. For we Jews are a people of symbol and type, and of the visual. The cloudy and fiery pillar, the curtain, the ark, the furnishings, the bread of the presence, the altar of incense, the priestly vestments—these were all given us because this is the language our hearts understand and respond to! So, this that we now do is representation only to assist recognition and understanding of how all is fulfilled in our wonderful Mashiach!"

He continued, making sure every eye was fixed and every mind attentive, "I will now go in there to demonstrate what the Great One, Yeshua our true High Priest, has once and for all accomplished and fulfilled in his very own body. As I enter that place, come with me, or see in your mind's eye, Yeshua entering the presence of Father Elohim—not as we do with the blood of that sacrifice—but with his very own blood, that of the Lamb of God who *takes away* the sin of the world and that was spilled in the fiery holocaust of Calvary for every one of us!"

The drama was intense.

"You see in this object lesson, or enactment," he said, "the atonement for your sin—his own blood—being carried in there, by him, your Great High Priest! And see, oh please do see the Father accept, yes, receive it, as sufficient—and then see the Father congratulate the Son as having accomplished what no other could . . . then to declare all of you reconciled to himself by this extraordinary act of Yeshua. Will you receive it? Receive it from the Father and from Yeshua! And then, those who have received may join in the new celebration of remembrance with the bread and with the wine—your celebration of the new covenant!

I and many in the waiting crowd bowed our heads and said a resounding, "Yes, I receive with thanks." And the priest entered, together with a throng . . . as I and others waited.

And then . . . ? Why then, the priest emerged again to make the declaration, and the people erupted in a mighty cheer and lifted their hands and hearts to heaven as the priest said, "Now go and live reconciled lives; live in it, receiving the peace of his forgiveness, and be reconciled to one another too. But before you go, join me in this new covenant 'feast' of bread and of wine to show that you have grasped and accepted and taken that life of his into yours."

And so, the people joined in great rejoicing and, then the token lamb, which had indeed been sacrificed, was spit roasted as a meal for the poor among them as though to distribute the very life of Yeshua to them.

This ceremony then began to be performed year by year as only Jewish people could perform it, with the garments of the high priest complete with all their adornments and the twelve precious stones. And part of the celebration was occupied by the one who played the part of the priest, representing Yeshua, explaining in detail the meaning of all the symbols and regalia as well as the various feasts. There were wonderful pictures on large screens and holograms and actors and music and commentary to headsets worn by all the visitors and participants who had indeed come from the four corners of the globe!

The Feast of Tabernacles, as well as the other Jewish feasts and Yom Kippur, were now dramas and visual spectacles played out annually for the benefit of the whole world. Included were dioramas and time lines and enactments and explanatory tours of the temple the Jews had built! The building of it, which had begun as an attempt to recapture the Old, had now miraculously, mysteriously, and marvelously led to discovery of the New! It was evangelism par excellence, now performed before a wondering world, which had heard of the great turning among the people known as the Jews. The gospel in glorious performance—and performed on the world stage by the very people through whom it came; beginning to end, the unfolding through time and history and people of the One called Mashiach . . . Mashiach for everyone. And the power of God descended on the drama so that it was greatly used to touch high and low the world over—and many met Mashiach there. In Jerusalem! Once more she was the center of the world's stage. It reminded many of what it must have been like in the days of the great Shalomoh when the kings and queens of the earth came to see the wonders of the city and the kingdom! Through God's ancient people once again was sounding out the message of redemption. Holiness unto the Lord was written everywhere, because hotels and facilities and cafes and restaurants had been dedicated to the glory and purposes of the Lord. And—because it was so, honesty abounded. Tourist traps and exploitative rip-offs had vanished, and leaders of nations were brought quickly to the conclusion that the more they aided and abetted and blessed what was occurring, the more their own lands and people were prospered and blessed! To say it was marvelous is understatement indeed, yet here it was—the words of the ancient prophet Zechariah unfolding for the world to behold . . . and to choose.

CHAPTER 13

The Fusion! (Part 2)

IN THE PREVIOUS CHAPTER we saw a storyline enabling us to imagine how some of Zechariah's foretelling might possibly play out—especially the words of Zech 12:10. It is an imagining only. It sometimes surprises us in the Scriptures to see how practically and simply words that would have been quite mysterious in prospect from a particular prophet's mouth and to the ears of hearers or readers about the life of Jesus—for example—were brought to pass and fulfilled. Think of the arrival of Mary and Joseph in Bethlehem because of a decree from Caesar Augustus for a census; or of Jesus riding into Jerusalem on a donkey; or about his death, burial, and resurrection. Matthew points out many of these fulfillments, which, once accomplished, were easily recognized in retrospect. Peter, at Pentecost had such an aha moment: "This is that," he cried, "which was spoken by the prophet Joel!"

It will be just the same for these as-yet-unfulfilled prophecies.

But, I want now to take us to the opposite side of the scenario—for if there is to be a fusion such as I am proposing, then we need to see that in that fusion, Christians will receive a heightened view and revelation of the wealth enshrined within Torah and Tanakh. Just as the truth of Jesus Christ as Mashiach will dawn for many Jewish people, many Christians will receive a revelation of the wholeness of God's word and plan.

Today, some Christians have become dismissive of the Old Testament; some, in the face of modern, carping, atheistic criticism, see the writings of the Old almost as an embarrassment. We have the so-called "new atheism" speaking loudly and vehemently of the "God who condones genocide, rape, and slavery." Of course, they are speaking from a position of gross ignorance and usually in the vain hope of getting the God of relentless pursuit out of their lives! They are both a product and a symptom of the age in which humanism reigns. The product is prideful humankind pretending to be far more righteous than this dreadful "god" of the Christians and their Bible. The behavior is a symptom—of fear. Fear that the God they shout so loudly to deny is, in fact, real—and will, in fact, have the last word. The loudness of their protest is in direct proportion to their fear that it may be so . . . or to a baleful hope that it is not!

New Cognizance

I have digressed! What will also come in this great fusion of which I am writing is a new recognition and embrace of the riches with which the old covenant is pregnant, by those now living within the new covenant, who have failed to appreciate that the written down word that God has given is a magnificent whole.

To be dismissive of the Old Testament is like cutting off the legs on which our torso stands.

Already today among Christians is a growing awareness of the almost inexhaustible depth of meaning within the Old. There are a growing number of messianic groups comprised of born-again Jewish believers, joined with non-Jewish Christians, who flow in deep appreciation of the feasts of the Jewish calendar and celebrate, for example, Pesach or Passover and Hag Shavuot (Pentecost) with all the richness that includes the sense of the anticipation within the Old and the joy of the "coming to pass" within the New.

In recent times those of the British Commonwealth have mourned the death of Queen Elizabeth II. There are many younger generations with little understanding of the richness of the traditions surrounding the monarchy—and hence see the trappings and the pomp and ceremony surrounding (for example) the queen's funeral as superfluous in our time. It is only when an appreciation of the meaning of the symbols is gained that the richness is appreciated. For example, we saw the symbols of monarchy—the crown, the scepter, the orb, which had been on the queen's coffin, surrendered to the head of the church and symbolically laid on the altar. This act is rich in meaning for it signifies the laying down of God-given rule, to the One from whom it came.

I will not paint a scene as I did in the last chapter. I hope my reader will catch the idea, that when, for example, a book has no prologue, the reader must pick up, as he or she proceeds, the stream of consciousness of the author and of the story. The prologue provides context and a platform, reveals what's happened to get the characters or the idea to the current moment. It enables the reader to launch into the book with some sense of where the journey begins, its expected trajectory, and where it will lead. In a real sense, for us on our part of the time line, the Old Testament is like the prologue. History has but one main event. Those who miss (or dismiss) the main event, will entirely miss the meaning of everything else and must invent philosophies and ideas to account for the human condition. The central events of the time line on which we live are Calvary and the resurrection. An appreciation of those facts and events is what brings everything else into focus and clarity. The Bible enables us to see the time line of history from above—the sky view. The central event has a before and an after— the "before" being the prologue and the "after" being the part of the story in which we live. The better understanding we have of the before, the greater our appreciation of the after—and of the whole.

In the Old, the nature, character, goodness, and methods of God are wonderfully disclosed. Not only that, but the nature, character, and failings of humankind, too, are disclosed!

I believe we will see a renewed discovery of the continuity of the Scriptures and even a repenting among some (perhaps many)

Christians for their neglect or even dismissive attitudes to the Old. Let it be, Lord!

Perhaps partly responsible for this neglect and ignorance has been that teaching emphasis of which I wrote in chapter 7, "Grace over against Grace," from John 1:16–17, which has made such a divide between the two—a divide that has engendered an awful view that God used to be harsh and vindictive, but now (fortunately for us) he's had a change of heart! This harmful view afflicts and impoverishes some Christians. As a Bible teacher I use the entire Bible, yet I had a clutch of folk in one church who complained that I used the Old too much. "We don't live there," I was told, "we are people of the New Testament . . . the Old has passed away." While Heb 8:13 tells us that the New has made the Old obsolete, the writer means it is obsolete as the means of access to God, not that it has no relevance to us. In fact, he goes forward, using the Old to illustrate and demonstrate the truths of what has now arrived. "The law," he says in ch. 10, was a shadow and not the image itself. Clearly, it could not, with its need for repetition of sacrifice, permanently deal with sin and "take away sins" as 10:4 and 11 inform us. However, the writer extensively uses people and illustrations from the Old to "color in" the New!

As Paul wrote in 1 Cor 10:6 and 11 of events in the Old, "Now these things *became our examples . . .*" and "*all these things* happened as examples and were written down *for our admonition* upon whom the ends of the ages have come."

We cannot do without them. They are part and parcel of the "package" provided us by the Father for our walk with him.

CHAPTER 14

"The Glory of Your People, Israel"
(Jesus, described by Simeon in Luke 2:19–32)

IN THE PREVIOUS TWO CHAPTERS I presented an imagining of a way in which the prophetic words of Zechariah and others might be fulfilled.

My purpose in the scenario of chapter 12 was an attempt to disperse the cloud of mystery that can shroud such prophecies and remind us that in the providence of God who moves all things, the fulfillment will, in retrospect, unfold with relative simplicity.

Now, as we've seen earlier, glory in the Bible means the substance and core of something. Both the Hebrew *khabod* in the Old Testament and δόξα (*doxa*) in New Testament Greek essentially relate to weightiness. We are apt to confuse glory with radiance. The glory of our nearest star, the Sun, is the trillions of tons of gas and nuclear activity of which it is comprised. Its radiance is the warmth and light emanating from that glory. This understanding is clearly demonstrated in Heb 1, where the writer describes Jesus as "the *radiance* of God's glory." Glory and radiance are not the same thing; glory is the producer, and radiance is the product.

So . . . when Simeon took the young child Jesus in his arms and said,

> Sovereign Lord, as you have promised,
> you may now dismiss your servant in peace.
> For my eyes have seen your salvation,
> Which you have prepared in the sight of all nations:
> A light for revelation to the Gentiles,
> and *the glory of your people Israel* (Luke 2:28–32 NIV)

. . . he was making a very significant statement.

In saying that his eyes had seen "*the glory* of your people Israel" he was saying that in seeing Jesus, he had seen Israel's core or essence—her substance and meaning! He was her raison-d'être; her purpose and reason for being were to produce Mashiach. He was "within" her life all the way along and constituted her "essence." "As a light to the Gentiles," God said typically in Isa 42:6 and 49:6. Through Malachi he said, "All the nations will call you blessed, for you will be a delightful land"—and so it goes in many further references.

The radiance or outshining of the "glory" within Israel—was to be (or was intended to be) her wisdom, light, and testimony to the nations.

The well-known "servant" passages of Isaiah bear this out as they can be considered as a description of the life of both the ideal Israel and the coming Mashiach.

Not only did national Israel largely miss or dismiss Yeshua when he came; she had been missing him, and her own very purpose and calling as his vehicle, much of the way along!

Had she focused less on imagined privilege and more on being who she was intended to be, things would have been different. Israel's behavior could be likened to an expectant mother complacently assured that the baby will one day arrive—all the signs were there—while entirely neglecting her own health, welfare, and preparation as integral to the pregnancy. Then, when the child arrived, Israel became like that same mother who post-birth had a bad case of maternal rejection of the child because of a distorted expectation. Mostly, with the exception of the few like Simeon, Israel missed the joy of childbirth—of bringing forth what she had herself been born for! This was a tragedy—but not one beyond redemption . . .

CHAPTER 15

"The Word of the Lord . . .
from Jerusalem"

IN CONCLUDING THIS BOOK, I want to bring us back to chapter 6, which was titled, "What the Prophets Saw." In that chapter I particularly referenced Isa 2 and Mic 4, where the same passage is used in describing what will come to pass in "the latter days."

I have always loved the biblical terms "it shall come to pass" and "it came to pass." They speak of certainty and, in fact, of inevitability. They assure us that what God has said will be; what is spoken from the eternal realm manifests in its perfect time, in the temporal and material realm.

Both Isaiah and Micah use the same words. Here they are from Isa 2:2–4 and Mic 4:1–3:

> Now it shall come to pass in the latter days
> That the mountain of the Lord's house
> Shall be established as the top[1] of the mountains,
> And shall be exalted above the hills;
> And all nations shall flow to it.
> Many people shall come and say,
> "Come, and let us go up to the mountain of the Lord,
> To the house of God, of Jacob;

---

1. Hebrew *rosh*, "on the head," meaning most important.

He will teach us His ways,
And we shall walk in His paths."
For *out of Zion shall go forth the law,*
And the word of the Lord from Jerusalem.
He shall judge between the nations,
And rebuke many people;
They shall beat their swords into plowshares,
And their spears into pruning hooks;
Nation shall not lift up sword against nation,
Neither shall they learn war anymore.

Biblically the "latter days" or "last" can broadly mean all that occurs after the saving work of Mashiach—his arrival, ministry, death, resurrection, and ascension. The writer of Hebrews, in Heb 1:1, uses the terms "former" and "last" in this way (as from the ISV translation):

> God, having spoken in *former times* in fragmentary and varied fashion to our forefathers by the prophets, has in these *last days* spoken to us by a Son whom he appointed to be the heir of everything and through whom he also made the universe.

(Paul also wrote similar things in both Rom 15:4 and 1 Cor 10:11.)

The "former" quite clearly refers to the old covenant era and the "last" or "latter" to the new covenant era and does mean that Christians need to exercise care when discussing what the Scriptures mean by latter days or last days. As I've indicated, in broad terms, it simply means history after Jesus Christ. We live in the latter days. How close to the "last day" we may only speculate, although world events as I write this in late 2023 appear to evidence some fulfillments and certainly momentum, pointing more clearly (and urgently) to that culminating "day"—the day of the Lord.

It is also evident that there have been, within this era of the "latter days," some preliminary or partial fulfillments of events foretold in the old era—a kind of "entrée" in spiritual terms for something that will enjoy a yet-to-come and more far-reaching and even physical realization. The partial came with, after, and following Messiah's (Mashiach's) first visit and his work on behalf of humankind. The final realization is to arrive as we draw close to his second and last appearing. After the first appearing the word of the Lord most certainly sounded out from Jerusalem, and at the personal level, he has already brought his peace to millions of surrendered hearts across the world and across the ages, but it appears there is to be an even greater "sounding out" of his word, yes, from Jerusalem, in days to come—at the culmination of these latter days.

My scenario in chapter 12 is only an imagining—but serves to illustrate a way in which that fulfillment could unfold. We can only imagine the impact on the entire world if, or when, such an awakening arises upon the Jewish people. I have illustrated how the world, in this age of social media and instancy, would see, hear, and know.

What is known is that at this present moment in history, the Temple Institute in Jerusalem is preparing all the necessary accoutrements for a new temple.[2] Not only are these preparations underway and advanced, but also a group of Jewish entrepreneurs have initiated plans to make Jerusalem a "world city" with a massive increase in available accommodation and facilities. The website of this influential group says, among much more, "Through proper long-term urban planning based on solid economic principles and benefits, Jerusalem 5800 will uncover Jerusalem's innate potential as a true 'World City' and tourist destination capable of attracting more than ten million tourists a year."[3]

It would appear the stage is being set for a new, unfolding drama—all the more reason for us to heed the words of David, "pray for the peace of Jerusalem" (Ps 122:6). And . . . to ensure our hearts and lives are forgiven, cleansed, and ready to meet King Jesus!

2. See https://templeinstitute.org/. Be sure to read the Statement of Principles in the "About" section of the site.

3. See https://www.jerusalem5800.com/.

CHAPTER 16

Paul Has the Last Word!

HAVING BEGUN WITH THE IDEA that the Hebrew zealot Saul becoming the Christian missionary Paul serves as an "archetype" of a much larger turning, it will be good to conclude by returning to him.

To his disciples Jesus had said, "I will not leave you as orphans, but will come to you" (John 14:18). And come he did, not long after his ascension, in the person of the Holy Spirit to both accompany and empower them for ministry. On the other hand, he said of unbelieving Jerusalem (and by extension, all whom she represented), "See! Your house is left to you desolate; for I say to you, you shall *see Me no more* until you say, 'Blessed is He who comes in the name of the LORD!'" (Matt 23:39).

These are starkly contrasting words to starkly contrasting audiences. On the one hand, a company of people who believed Jesus to be the promised Messiah and were following him. He was preparing them for what would be the harrowing trial of his coming death and departure to his Father. On the other hand, a larger group who were indifferent to and dismissive of the truth—and would soon cry, "Away with him!" One would experience comfort and, indeed, have a profound sense of being "gathered" under his wings and in no sense "orphaned." The other, having spurned him, would miss out and experience a period of isolation or desolation—which brings us back to Paul and Rom 11—where he reminds us (in v. 29) that the "gifts and the calling of God are *irrevocable*"! This means, as he explains, that in the extraordinary "depths of the wisdom and knowledge of God," he is able to graft back in the natural branches of the olive tree—providing they don't continue in unbelief. Just as the "wild olive" branches get grafted in by faith—that is, when they believe—so too the way back in for the "broken off" natural branches is by faith!

To return to the revelation of Paul seeing himself as firstfruits and a kind of archetype of a regrafted Israel, let me say the following: He was part and parcel and typically representative of the temporarily "broken off" and "set aside" Israelite people. His spirit had been the same spirit as the mob that had vehemently cried, "Away with him!" Yet, although broken off and, in that sense, desolate, the hand of God was still sovereignly upon this Saul of Tarsus, governing, arranging, and ensuring the fulfillment of a grand plan—as well as of a great typifying! What could and did happen to a Saul of Tarsus could just as surely occur in the life of his "broken-off" people! And will. And indeed is occurring.

Sing, O Daughter of Zion!

The hand of God remains sovereignly upon his temporarily "broken-off" branches. Like Israel in her desolate wilderness years, God, though displeased with their unbelief, was nonetheless sovereignly watching, taking care, protecting, and providing. She had suffered those forty wilderness years because of unbelief—her failure to enter and appropriate what her Lord had promised her. So, today, Israel suffers because she would not allow him to "gather" her so that they became distinctively his by recognizing and appropriating him as their Mashiach. Nonetheless, in her current wilderness he cares, provides, and protects—and little by little, is indeed, gathering. Many are coming to recognition and coming under his wings.

In the scenario presented in this book, I have provided a picture of how a great company of those among this people of God's election might find themselves "regrafted" by faith, into the Tree. As and when this occurs, we may just have one of those collective aha moments such as that of Peter at Pentecost when we say, "*This is that* which was spoken by the prophet Zechariah."

I will leave the reader pondering some words of Zephaniah and Isaiah . . .

Sing, O daughter of Zion! Shout, O Israel!
Be glad and rejoice with all your heart, O daughter of
Jerusalem!
The Lord has taken away your judgments, He has cast out
your enemy.
The King of Israel, the Lord, is in your midst; You shall see
disaster no more.
In that day it shall be said to Jerusalem: "Do not fear; Zion,
let not your hands be weak.
The LORD your God is among you; He is mighty to save.
He will rejoice over you with gladness; He will quiet you
with His love;
He will rejoice over you with singing."
"I will gather those among you who grieve over the ap-
pointed feasts,
so that you will no longer suffer reproach.
Behold, at that time, I will deal with all who afflict you.
I will save the lame and gather the scattered;
and I will appoint praise and fame for the disgraced
throughout the earth.
At that time, I will bring you in; yes, at that time I will
gather you.
For I will give you fame and praise among all the peoples of
the earth
when I restore your captives before your very eyes."
(Zeph 3:14–20)

But Israel shall be saved by the LORD with an everlasting
salvation;
You shall not be ashamed or disgraced forever and ever.
(Isa 45:17)

APPENDIX

Artist's impression of Jebus, which David took and renamed the city of
David, and showing the walled enclosure surrounding the Gihon Spring.
The knob or prominence to the north is where the Dome of the Rock shrine
stands today. Image Courtesy of City of David Archives of Ancient Jerusalem
Creator: Orfan
Used with permission